Celebrative Anthology by the **POETS of INDIANA**

James Whitcomb Riley (1849-1916)

Riley in Memoriam

— James Whitcomb Riley

John H. Morgan, editor

Wyndham Hall Press

RILEY IN MEMORIAM

A Celebrative Anthology by the Poets of Indiana

James Whitcomb Riley (1849 – 1916)

John H. Morgan, Editor

Illustrations reprinted by permission from
Hubert M. Eitel, the son of Edmund Eitel,
a close friend of Riley for many years.

§ Publishing since 1877,
Bristol Banner Books is the poetry imprint of
Wyndham Hall Press, Inc.

Library of Congress
Catalog Card Number
89-040432

ISBN 1-55605-099-2 (hardback)
ISBN 1-55605-100-X (paperback)

THE POET IN THE PRIME OF LIFE

In recognition of the admiration
James Whitcomb Riley
held for America and the Presidency,
this book is
DEDICATED TO THE LIVING PRESIDENTS
OF THE UNITED STATES OF AMERICA.

RICHARD M. NIXON

GERALD R. FORD

JIMMY (James Earl) CARTER

RONALD W. REAGAN

GEORGE BUSH

Legislative Sponsor of the Poets of Indiana

The Honorable Representative
Donald T. Nelson, Ph.D.
Indianapolis, Indiana

EDITOR'S NOTE

On the occasion of the sesquicentennial of the birth of James Whitcomb Riley, Wyndham Hall Press is pleased to bring before the reading public a collection of contemporary poems written by poets, both established and aspiring, of Indiana.

These poems merely reflect the enduring regard with which Riley is held in today's literary community. A man of talent and a citizen nurtured by a love for his country and his people, James Whitcomb Riley continues to embody in his literary legacy a breadth of sympathy and depth of subtlety indicative of his greatness.

At a time in history when language is too often thought to be merely a political medium for dominance and manipulation, it seems appropriate that a resolute affirmation of the beauty and truthfulness of language be celebrated. How better to celebrate the grandeur of language than in a poetic celebration to James Whitcomb Riley, Hoosier extraordinaire.

John H. Morgan, Ph.D., D.Sc.(London)   Poetry Editor
Wyndham Hall   Bristol, Indiana
Autumn   1989

CONFUSION

My heart is with me
In it's proper place
My soul has left me

Life seems jubilant
But I feel empty
My thoughts are with me
I feel lonely

Time goes slowly
So many thoughts
Tear through my heart
Water stings my eyes

Wanting Heaven
Fearing Hell
Needing life
Frightened of death

Penny Almy
Vincennes

THE GIFT

God gave me a gift on your birthday-
A child to teach me how to love.
You, to lead me back to him-
A sweet perfect gift from above.

I had wandered far from him,
My heart was cold as stone.
It took you to take me back-
A task for you alone.

I wanted this for you, I said
To teach these tiny lips to pray,
for you to have a friend in Jesus
As I had in my childhood days.

But as I took you to learn from Him,
He called me to His side
He said He sent you to the earth
For you to be my guide.

So back on the path my feet are drawn,
And I have a long way to go.
But with my child, my gift from God
To guide me, I'll make it-I know.

                    Cathy Alsman
                    Sullivan

MY CALL

You may be called to be a preacher, or to be a classroom
    teacher
You may be an enforcer of the law.
You may be a missionary, or some kind of visionary,
But my calling is the best of all -
I'm a Grandmaw.

I get to go back and be a child, and do things that's fun and
    wild,
Like seeing who is quickest on the draw.
We play we're "super friends" and other "let's pretends".
The greatest call of all -
Is being a Grandmaw.

I read books by the dozens, as I rock these charming cousins,
These are the greatest kids you ever saw,
We swing and we blow bubbles, and I forget about my troubles.
It really is a ball -
Being a Grandmaw.

I don't think I could be the other - I mean, a Grandmother.
that sounds like it would be no fun at all.
I'm glad I've had a chance, to sing and laugh and dance,
And enjoy this lofty call -
Of being a Grandmaw.

                            A. Rebecca Ammerman
                            Westport

MAGIC WORD MACHINE

I have a magic word machine
That's deep within my mind.
It always treats me tenderly,
it always treats me kind.
So when I'm blue
or down and out,
my word machine
will bring me out.
It brings out the sun on a rainy day,
and when I am sad it makes me gay.
My greatest wish that could ever come true,
is that everyone else could have it too.

Stephen F. Atkinson
Logansport

THE PREDICAMENT OF
THOMAS WENTWORTH HIGGINSON
IN REGARD TO EMILY DICKINSON

In 1862 when Thomas Wentworth Higginson, 19th century critic, received a letter from Emily Dickinson, in which she shared some of her poems with him, he probably thought...

"Melodic...delicate...
    but no form...
Remarkable...
    but imperfectly rhymed.
Words flow...
    but a spasmodic beat...
Range of theme...yes...
Dimensions of time...
    and beautiful thoughts...
    but still..."

Professor Higginson,
caught
halfway between "awe" and "odd"
in walls too small to recombine
What-Was with What-Could-Be,
    pondered the new creation...
    and simply said,

"Nice, Emily,
but NOT for publication."

Hope Barnes
Muncie

LIGHTNING WHELK

A shell! I'm holding it here, in my hand
Tossed up in a wave's furious rush to the sand

From some distant shore, on the incoming tide.
A sea creature's discarded home, cast aside.

Unwanted, now useless, no value upon it
Be it cowrie, or cockle, or oyster, or bonnet.

Expended, it lay there, for all plain to see
Until it was picked up, by you, just for me.

A shell! What a trifle! Flotsam of the shore.
To me it is treasure, unwanted no more.

No limpet could cling to the rock it grew near
Nor barnacle fasten itself to the pier

With greater tenacity, through sea and sand,
Than I cling to the shell that you put in my hand.

Dorothy B. Barrett
Zionsville

JAMES WHITCOMB RILEY

This is the anniversary of James Whitcomb Riley's birth.
His poems were full of mirth.
He was called the Hoosier Poet
Because he wrote about Indiana and his poems show it.
Mr. Riley wrote stories about the Raggedy Man
And about Orphan Ann.
Some of his poems are sad,
But they aren't bad.
What I like most
Is the story about the ghost.

Buster Basenfelder
Lafayette

IN SILENCE:
memories of Sachsenhausen 50 years later

Temperature below freezing, snow on the ground,
In the midst a man collapses, not wanting tomorrow,
Judged by those he never knew, he remembers their verdict;
    We will show him no mercy,
    His crimes are unspeakable,
    He shows no remorse,
    He is guilty of "love",
    He is father of nothing,
    His life is a zero,
    His ways are a sin,
    We will give him a purpose,
And here he waits scarcely clothed, soaking wet, chained to a
    pole,
Those who show care are beaten to near death,
Those who can help are marked if they dare,
With the last breath from his pneumonic lungs he whispers;
    Judge them as persons,
    Show them some mercy,
    Open their eyes,
    Let them see -what -they're --doing

The evidence was removed in silence.

                        Jeffrey Gene Bass
                        Bloomington

GOIN' TO GRAN-MA'S

I remember when goin' to Gran-ma's meant the country;
An' the chickens, an' the crick, an' that ol' climbin' tree.
An' there's no forgettin' that house fillin' smell -
Comin' from the kitchen, when Gran-ma made bread.
I remember that post with the dinner bell,
That all within hearin' it would tell,
It's time to stop, an' come an' eat!
Then us kids would race, to see who beat.
There was a pan by the pump an' a towel on the line,
An' that ol' lye soap sure make you shine.
Then we'd sit to a meal, surely fit for a King!
Then down to the crick with a piece of string an' bent pin,
We'd just lay back, waitin' for the fun to begin.
Goin' to Gran-ma's - I'll never forget!
An' often in dreams, I'm out there yet.

Omer J. Beals, Jr.
Gas City

"QUEST"

I sit and ponder what to do.
My every thought is crowding through.
Oh, Lord, Where is the reason, the quest for truth?
In son, daughter, brother, mother, sister, father? What's the
    use?
Even if I find the answer the greater truth.
It will not last, nothing is permanent you see.
For the answer right now, tomorrow may not be.

I sit and ponder what to do.
He was so handsome, quite free at heart.
I gave all I had at the very start.
But then he took what I so freely gave.
And misused, abused, my thoughts gave me no chance.
To protect myself, to learn of him, to grow with him.
To protect myself for reaching out.

I sit and wonder what to do.
Wondering, caring, trying not to fret.
There is a answer, clearly defined.
Then I look at the homeless, the hungry too.
Oh, if everyone helped, so many would pull through.
A chance to change their lives and begin anew.
There is an answer, I know it now, It's me and It's you.

                              Martha Beamon
                              Fort Wayne

RAINBOWS AND ROSES

After a soft summer shower, a beautiful rainbow glowed for
  an hour
I heard it say that there would be a blessing for the gentle
  hearted
Then appeared the roses to me glistening with raindrops just
  departed
With long graceful stems that swayed in the breeze
They whispered to each other secrets a rose only sees

Purple, red and blue grace the rainbow's hue
Arching high up in the sky where the stormy rainclouds lie
And after the rain is o'er, sunshine comes knocking at my
  door
Then I smell the roses' scent that the summer's shower has
  lent
Satiny soft a rose is gowned with colors bright she is crowned

Rainbows and roses make a beautiful pair
Both are lovely in the colors they share
They show a kind gentleness after the rain
Calling to each other as they nod a refrain
The roses open their petals so fair and talk to the rainbow way
  up there
"Mr. Rainbow, I thought that you should know,
You put on a really spectacular show."

The rainbow looked down with mists in his eyes,
"Miss Rose, said he, you'll win first prize
For your beauty's so rare a thing to behold
It is surely more precious than silver or gold"
It touches the rose and gives new birth
Now when the rainbow stretches to earth,
To the beauty of life in God's magnificent creation
Rainbows and roses share total elation

Delene Montogomery Beaty
Tipton

PEBBLES IN THE SAND

All the emotion conveyed in the brushing of two hands,
   the accidental meeting of eyes, the sympathetic smile
All the fear when a stranger passing by
   hides her eyes and looks at the sky, beads scattered
   on the floor
All the love of whispered words

All the innocence of a small child singing, of an old woman
   crying
All the beauty of a gnarled tree, the mournful melodies of a
   dying swan
All the courage and cowardice in my heart coalesced to tie
   a knot in coherence
The anticipation of a fleeting touch, soon over but long
   remembered
The pain of a noble promise soon forgotten

All the desperate questions and lonely answers

Pebbles in the sand.

               Robby Behrman
               Huntington

SUMMER ENCHANTMENT

Remember the coin that I found in the sand,
A treasured memento to hold in my hand?
It speaks of July with a torrid hot sun,
Of swimming at leisure and bodies "well done"!
Convertible rides and a bright summer moon,
Star-gazing 'til morning, a popular tune.
Some hot dogs and buns with potato chips, too,
Cupcakes and kool-aid, we went to the zoo.
Then later when clouds were fluffy and white,
County fairs thrilled us from morning to night.
A ride on the bobs was my favorite of all.
You held me so tight, so that I wouldn't fall.
At ninety degrees, most people don't go,
But we were in love, and we didn't know!
We reached for a star a-top our sand dune,
That Hoosier-hot summer, which ended too soon!

Charlotte Faber Bendt
Crown Point

"A BICYCLE RIDE"

"Ain't she funny? Biscuits and Britches ridin' on a pony.
Tain't right you know. She been treadin' ground for a long
while!" But in the middle of the street heard a voice and a
sound quite mixed with relief. "Sssh! somethin's a comin!"
Drowning out the voice won't help Buttercup!" But it's
still night!" "I know, and we be knowin' it too!" And then
they watched as the voice filled pager gave way to the
streets, and spoke not nary a word. Only sirens seen and
felt. "Jumpin, breadin, treadin, hopin', helpful, handful is
me! I gotta wash dem clothes for the night!" And with that
she applauded the verse...

Charles A. Beyer, Jr.
Westfield

A MOTHER'S LOVE!

Is the richest kind
It gives a child
Peace of mind
A mother's love **never** sleeps
No matter how grown you are
When trouble comes
Upon her child
A mother **isn't** too proud to weep!
A mother's love is understanding
A mother's job is demanding
Motherhood is a twenty-four hour a day
Seven day a week undertaking
So, every mother alive today
Deserves the Best!
After all it's **not just** her children
That put her to a test!

Sally F. Bishop
Indianapolis

FALL

Tears and cheers
Bittersweet climbing
Sunflowers shriveled
Apples falling
Frosty breath
Leaves whispering
Oh - snow
Too late

Pat Blenner
Elkhart

MY TIE, MY TIE, MY BEAUTIFUL TIE

Shades of yellow and green you know,
Three inches wide and all aglow.
I don't know why they would look amazed,
It was as though they were in a daze.
I picked this tie and wore it with pride,
They snickered and laughed and turned aside.
Who are they to be the judge?
I love my tie, I will not budge.
I'll keep it forever I want you to know,
    My tie--my tie--it will not go.
    So no one else can snicker with glee,
    I'll not wear my tie for them to see.
    Oh no! you'll never see my tie again,
    I'm taking it with me when Jones' tucks me in.

                Ruth M. Bole
                Van Buren

REEDS IN THE WIND

As the reeds sway to and fro,
With the wind and back,
Often whipped to stinging force
Many bend and crack!
I, too, brace the winds of life;
Bow to meet their force,
Only to be tossed again
On a smoother course.
While the winds blow wild and free,
Reeds and I meet destiny!

Gwen Roberts Boyer
Dyer

THE PLEADING SOUL

Lord Jesus, enter into my heart.
I beg of thee, O Lord,
Give me a new start.

I am tired of walking this life alone.
For my sins, only you,
O Lord, can atone.

I know to Jesus I must turn,
or in hell,
I will surely burn.

So Lord, enter into my heart.
For from this old life,
I must now depart.

My spirit is bleeding.
My body is in death,
And my soul is pleading,
For you O Lord.

On this day, I pray,
O Lord, that my sins,
You wash away, and
My body to be cleansed.
　　　　　　　Amen.

　　　　　　Elmer Bradus
　　　　　　Salem

LIFE GOES ON

The great old oak tree
that grew in the front yard
with its long, wide-spread branches
cast its regal shadow upon the house.

Winters came and winters went
years of snow and ice had took its toll.
For one spring day, the birds sang
but no new sprouts or sprigs of leaves grew.

The great old oak had given up.
There would be no nests for the birds,
no more hide 'n seek for the squirrels,
no regal shadow upon the house.

A crew came to take the great oak away.
The sound of thunder was heard and the rains came.
It rained for days, suddenly from among the clouds appeared
    the sun
its rays of light and warmth gave life to a new oak tree.

                    Marcia Brauer
                    North Vernon

THE WHITE SEEDS

Saturdays, before Dad would mow the grass,
We would run through the ragged yard, still wet
With morning mist, picking up rocks, tree limbs,
And neighbors' trash; and then, we would all get

Long sticks and, swinging them like saw-toothed scythes,
Cut off the heads of dandelions, both
The bright, wheat-ripe scalps and those ghost-white ones
That got windswept and scattered, like frayed cloth

Tossed from a truck cab, westbound in Texas.
Last week, my son and I played catch at Flott
Park, in a field of weeds flowering in dirt
The color of an asphalt parking lot.

Once, when Dan lobbed the ball deep, I dropped back
And bobbled it till it rolled past a dead
Tree, stopping among rotting dandelions.
Then wind blew and once more I saw the seeds

Floating through green branches above our lawn;
Once more it was May when we breathed the gray
Smoke of grass-cutting, when no one knew life
Could end, even while watching white seeds float away.

Matthew Brennan
Terre Haute

CORDUROY TIME

The moon wears a maizey haze
to make me think of autumn days.
A view of turquoise, rust or wine.
Toast and plum produce a sign
of the corduroy time of year.

Wearing all those little grooves,
tempts each finger as it moves,
to feel the coat or suit or dress.
Across its hills and valleys press,
in the corduroy time of year.

But what one really often ponders,
as the hand so freely wanders,
Is "was that interest always there?",
yet touching one just would not dare
til the corduroy time of year.

(end)

Joyce Brinkman
Indianapolis

"THE MIND"

I wonder sometime about the mind,
    about the thoughts of others.

What says misuse, abuse, neglect
    in minds of our own mothers?

How would you calm the restless mind,
    the racy, noisy, restless mind?

The one who calms the raging sea,
    will also calm the rage in me.

Is that where hatred got its start,
    what signals vileness to the heart?

How do you erase ignorance from the mind,
    the vast, unyielding, restless mind?

I wonder sometime, about the mind...

                    Neva Brooks-Harrington
                    Indianapolis

BORN THIRTY YEARS TOO SOON

Did you ever meet a feller
Born thirty years too soon?
I mean just a feller
Who was always out of tune.
Did you ever watch his actions,
And feel the right to say,
"He's a little too high-minded
To be here anyway."

When he talked of running engines
and cars with solar rays,
Did you just say, "He's crazy!"
And go right on your way?
Did you ever see him gazin'
And lookin' at the moon,
And say, "He's just a feller
Born thirty years too soon."?

Mary Zoe Sager Brown
Cayuga

A CHID

A bulb we plant for channels of our lives
To nurture and feed but of our own
To love and hold through sorrow or laughter
Yesterday was but only a fragment
Tomorrow is the rest of its life
The sickly child that must fight for his own
To scientist his fate is unknown
But to all and everyone of us his smile goes on
The pain and suffering for which it stands
My child if only I could take you home
I'd watch you grow each day that goes by
Oh my child your little mind
How I wish the pain and suffering was mine.

                    Pamela J. Brown
                    Carmel

THE PROGRESSION OF CIVILIZATION
REVEALED IN A ROOM

Our primitivism is primitive tamed.
This self-awareness needn't be defamed.
For we linger much in one room:
A civil jungle with a fetid fume.
And water pours daily there
Like water under Nature's care.
Its purging rain in temperatures fall,
Removing dust from clay, and that's all.
But within junglewater thoughts we find.
Although connotations go undefined.
So junglewater have upon us imposed
Thoughts from which history's composed.
The essence of self, then, is never removed.
Yes, primitivism is merely primitive reproved.

Reginald V. Bruster
Vincennes

PASSIN' DOWN THE RILEY RHYMES

I grew up with Riley poems
That my Mama read to me
And my brothers as we gathered
To be read to 'round her knee.

"Knee-deep in June" brought pictures
Of the lane we lived along
And Bryant's Creek was "Brandywine,"
When she read us that song.

We saw fodder shocks and punkins
And turkeys that we raised
As she read from the pages
'Bout the Hoosier land he praised.

Then, to all our children, Grandma
Read lots of Riley rhymes
Like stories the "Raggedy Man" told
"If we be good sometimes."

Now Mama's gone, but my grandkids
By my knees gather 'bout
For tales of things that happen
To folks who "don't watch out."

We're so glad the Hoosier Poet
Left the rhymes we love so much---
James Whitcomb Riley blessed us
With his special down home touch!

                    Emma Jane Buis
                    Martinsville

THE ARRIVAL OF AUTUMN

Bright blue skies darkened to leaden gray,
   The sun seemed to don a frown;
Northwest Wind sounded his trumpet loud
   And the leaves came rustling down.

The Maples answered with scarlet and gold,
   The giant Oaks kept their brown;
Such a gorgeous flurry filled the air
   As the leaves came tumbling down.

The bright storm moved with varying pace
   Through streets and alleys in town;
Now high, now low, now fast, and then slow
   As the leaves came scurrying down.

Then sullen raindrops fell and fell on
   The bright blanket on the ground;
Now there are drifts of several hues
   Since the leaves came twirling down.

Stella Taylor Burge
North Vernon

NORTHERN LIGHTS

His home was wheeled, rounded, and doorless;
he kept the keys in the ignition
and wine in the refrigerator.
He believed in peace pipes but smoked cigars
for the same reason children ran.

They had a holographic relationship;
cataclysmal caresses melted chocolate fireworks -
they played with lightning like
wild white dancers.

She
was an island-blue-eagle person who
showed him Indian dawns and
cliffs of fire that he'd remembered from prior lives.

He
took her diving for sundrops
and taught her to seek hidden roads and
walk with surprise.

His passion made him move like
jazz on a griddle 'cos he knew

she
was the best memory he'd ever
pulled out of his hat.

                    Kathryn Smith Burnett
                    Mishawaka

RECALL

As a child, I slept, but did not dream;
I played and didn't know what I was playing;
and I smelled the sweet scents of youth,
but I didn't take notice.
But somewhere deep inside my mind, I
was storing all of these stimuli for
a later use...
Then...
As an adult, I dream, and most of the
time they are wonderful dreams of child-
like visions.
I work, and can remember to the minutest
detail, the games of my youth.
And I can pick a scent out of a world
of hate and despair and connect it with
a period of childhood innocence...
...I must be growing old.

                    Dave Burton
                    Morgantown

A WINTER MORNING

A winter morning, cold, crisp, clean
Outside there is a dazzling scene
Of snow covered trees and mystical shapes
As if bushes and fences had pulled their drapes
And settled down to sleep.

Children in parkas and mittens feel led
By an inner call to find a sled
And trudge merrily through each cotton-like mound
To that special hill that someone found
Where the snow gets ever so deep.

The snow is tramped by foot and hand
As the course the sleds will take is planned,
Then sleds line up in a zig zag train
And down they go again and again
To erringly land in a heap.

The morning flies by at a rapid pace
With joy reflected on each child's face
As though he knows, in a grown up way,
That he will treasure this winter's day
In memory to keep.

Dolores Cains

LaPorte

LAMENTATION

"Ah, Rufin, Rufin, come down from heaven, boy;
There's those here needs yuh."
He wept, the old man, gaunt and bent,
Not wanting to be a supplicant,
His voice beseeching if he could
Return the boy to the place he'd stood.
"If someone's up there, mebbe God,
You know my askin' be not so odd.
This here's Bertha's child;
Her reprieve
From a dozen stillborn she conceived.
We're all alone, sir. We have naught
Save this here boy my Bertha begot.
What's livin' nohow if you ain't
Got no one to touch; it makes you faint.
Yuh tuk him so quick I fergit
Whuther I told him I loved him yit.
His Ma expects him.
Supper's on.
How will I tell her
That Rufin's gone?"

                              Camarshall
                              Culver

MAY

May!

Beneath the shade of a blooming tree, I lay
Sweet smell of blossoms lingering all day.

The fresh smell of new life enlivens me
I smile and stretch to touch the sun.

Care-free and child-like, I run
Giggling happily, having fun.

The warm sun and cool breeze touch my spirit
I lay down in nature's blanket of love.

Of everlasting May mornings, I dream
As the sun's rays glisten off the stream.

My heart is light my spirit lifts
As I sit and dream beneath the blooming tree.

                    Leslie C. Camp
                    Hammond

OUR HOOSIER STATE

It's Indiana where the corn grows tall,
And wheat sways in the breeze like a synchronized wall;
Where apples hang heavy in the fall;
Yes, Indiana's the best state of all!

In Daviess County the melons grow sweet;
And there are coal mines to harvest for winter heat;
And always a prolific, steady flow
Of oil from the sub-surface far below!

Contented cows provide meat and cream;
Our larders literally burst at the seams.
Rivers and lakes provide fish and play
When it's time to get away for a day.

Whatever your hobbies, you needn't go far,
Take a plane or a train, or drive your car!
We've Little League, and professional ball,
And our youngsters, like corn, grow ten feet tall!

Now there's conservation at parks and zoos,
And our history reads like a book of "Who's Who"!
We have politicians and astronauts, too;
And famous musicians from old I.U.

We travel the world, but we come back home.
There's no better place on earth to roam;
For God made Indiana self-sufficient and free!
Hoosier hospitality invites you. Come see!

Alice S. Campbell
Lafayette

DOWN THE ALLEY

"If you don't stay clean," they'd say
"we'll give you to the rag man."
But in the alley no one told me
not to climb the trash barrel
onto the rungs of the splintery pole
or hide in the weeds where I studied
the pebbled shine of flat tin cans,
watched a stray dog for mouth foam,
ate the wild rhubarb by the fence.

No one knew I stalked the rag man
with his mule and wooden cart, crying
"any old raaags, paperrrs, iron-to-sell,"
or heard me stop him and run
for the drawstring bag of my grandmother's
dirty laundry and take his dime.
But they found me watching
as he creaked away, his iron wheels
biting the rocks, his gritty song
calling--me with the coin warm
in my fist, touched by his black-
creased hand, the fingers that drove
the dusty mule back where everything
was scrap and rags and dirt.

                    Mike Carson
                    Evansville

LITTLE GIRL'S FANTASY

My name was
    Julia Winifred Riley.
I was a Hoosier, too,
    Alas! not a poet -
    Well, not much of one!
But, I've always loved
    Our Hoosier Poet.
His "Little Orphant Annie"
Sent chills up and down
    My small girl spine!
And I read in rapture,
"When The Frost Is On The Punkin."
"That Old Sweetheart Of Mine" could
Take my sympathizin' heart
    Right down its soulful lines!
I knew he couldn't be
    My grandfather;
    He never married.
But I always said he was,
    "My uncle."
I was proud, too, our names were
    So much alike:
JAMES WHITCOMB RILEY
JULIA WINIFRED RILEY

                    Julia Winifred Riley Carter
                    Marion

TO A LADY

It was as though a flower
Had found a voice -- her petals
Lilting of fragility, complexity,
Importuning dumbly of the value of
Her own transience --
Speaking silently against the sun
And even against water -- as though
The lack of them made her more beautiful,
And age had become her good friend -- and
As I looked at her standing by the Seine,
I understood death and tyranny,
And I preferred death --

S. M. Chilcote
Knox

STRINGING THE BOW

"...like a musician, like a harper when
with quiet hand upon his instrument
he draws between his thumb and forefinger
a sweet new string upon a peg: so effortlessly
Odysseus in one motion strung the bow."
                    --The Odyssey, Book XXI

It takes a long time to learn what not to say.
You will wander for twenty years,
live among strangers, mimic their ways,
and you will sit alone staring at the sea,
naked and tired as a rock,
you will squat on the sand,
sun and rain, waiting and listening,
until you know what home is,
and how to get there,
and whose voice you need to hear when you arrive.

Tell your son none of this at journey's end.
He must blister his own hands
to find it out for himself,
or not at all.
When you teach, what you say is the least of it.
What will bend, will bend to your back
and your hands and your heart.
Musician, magician, father:
you string the bow
and then let go.

                    Roger A. Chrastil
                    Mishawaka

RAINBOW CHILD

Pausing before the bare canvas
I hesitate, not speaking,
Not allowing the feeling.

Yet, the sweet child in me
Who longs for the rich color of life,
Knowing the flavor without having tasted
Moves toward the canvas with caution.

Arms rigid, fearful of spilling
Out some darkness of the past
A history you do not know
And may not care to meet.
I dare not move.

But the whiteness invites me
Openly
To splash upon it
All the beauty I hold inside
And I present you a rainbow ...me.

E. Patterson Church
Bloomington

TRACKS

we walked along the same track
between the rails and spikes
each taking short broken steps
following the pattern of the ties below
occasionally losing balance
stepping on the jagged rocks surrounding
i'm tired of this walk he said
so leaning on my shoulder
he climbed on top of
the rail
we walked along the same track
me still following the same path
he walking unsteadily
on top of the rail
why are you having so much trouble i asked
he said because i keep looking back

Kenneth Alan Clarke
Ft. Wayne

IN HIS HOLY WRIT

In His Holy Writ,
Jesus asked a living sacrifice;
Our total body, that was it,
Nothing less would e'er suffice.

So I gave Him it;
Including all my mental power
A holy, sacrificial gift
His to use each day and hour.

Help me Lord to give
Your love, your special care,
That others evermore may live
Your home in Heaven to share.

Olive L. Coleson
Marion

PRAYING FOR OTHERS

Open their eyes that they may see
    The glorious future God has for you and me.
Open their ears that they may hear
    The many promises He has prepared.

Give them a glimpse of what can be theirs
    When they accept Jesus, and his life do share,
To guide and direct them in their daily walk
    And enjoy his fellowship as you talk.

Praying to God, in Jesus' Name, and always being
    Faithful and in Him trust -------
Is the best answer because we know
    That Jesus is always fair and always just.

We're to pray for our loved ones and enemies too
    Because that's what Jesus did and wants us to do.
"Pray for those over us", He says
    "Pray for those in Government and leadership places";

This helps them to make decisions best for all
    And keeps this a Nation Under God and recall
That God is in charge, and we can lean on Him,
    Because God knows what is best and we believe in HIM.

               Gladys Collins
               Orland

DANCER OF THE NIGHT

You came at night under a reflecting light
In search of self, you move rhythmically to
the music of your soul
I felt myself a part of your song
Dancer of the night, what is your name?

Are you the movement of the trees?
The motion of the waters stirring within?
I feel the presence of many calling
Come with us, be a part of the song
Dancer of the night, what is your name?

I am here by choice
I don't know how to dance to your song
Limitations of awareness holds you, Let go
You are Loved, come dance with us,
for we are you
Dancer of the night, what is your name?
Yours is ours, it's the same

Elizabeth Conklin
Indianapolis

PATAGONIA

"Who has time to shop? Call now!"
                              gurgles the Poisoner
        as in ancient rhyme
        and timeless knock
a handful of white sails
timid wakes at their tails
        toil through the Land of Great Feet.
            Amid the screech of midnight fires
        in poisonous districts dense
intensely vain
but whorishly sane
the crews move on
        twisting reason into poison.
Now from the miasma i see:
            We the Poisoned set the global duty
            and then couldn't pay the fare
            Visa-expediting services now
            if you're too busy to care

            And Magellan's head on the beach
            looking east in the heat
            sweat mixed with palm wine
            and promise in his matted hair.

                        John K. Cox
                        Bloomington

A CHANGE OF LIFE

When I go back to my home and I walk through the door, to
    my surprise I see,
That my family is no longer any more, the way that they used
    to be.
But I thought to myself, "Oh how can this be?
Everyone is so different except for me!"
My brother and two sisters have loved ones of their own.
And here I sit, and I feel so alone.
We shared so much -- our laughter and tears...
Has this really disappeared through the years?
I listen to everyone talk and I sigh,
I feel so left out, and I start to cry.
I long for the days when everyone cared.
Is this just a phase, that I'm feeling so scared?
Have they really all changed except for me?
Have I gone through changes that I don't see?
At college I'm away from everyone, too.
So is there any justice for my feeling blue?
My brother is happy, my sisters just glow;
They all seem so wise and know just where to go.
So when I return to my corner to sit, full of doubt and feeling
    blue...
I begin to realize after thinking a bit, that I wouldn't change a
    thing, would you?

                              Kristina Crabtree
                              Indianapolis

JAMES WHITCOMB RILEY

To the summit of Crown Hill I've climbed
For inspiration, at Riley's grave.
Though he died before my birth,
I feel a kinship near this earth.

The autumn colors paint his tomb
The marble pillars, softer seem;
And amber leaves have rustled near,
To kiss the steps around the bier.

I hope perchance, by being here,
This honored, highest site in town,
That thoughts he had so long ago,
Might in me, somehow, start to flow.

In him, all mankind had a friend
As from a thousand poems he penned,
The heart of him was clear to all
Who read his lines from start to end.

When people hear of Riley's name,
They only think of him as "Poet",
But poetry was just a way,
That he portrayed his time of day.

The greatness of the man is seen,
Within his writings o'er the years.
His love of nature, life and man,
Were themes which through his poems ran.

Were it not for his great gift,
To versify romance with life,
His name would not now be revered,
Nor his poems in our hearts endeared.

Josef Dahlstrand, Jr.
Indianapolis

FOR MOTHER

Dearest Mother
If I could give you
On Mother's Day
A giant bouquet
Of bright lavender...pink...
I would give you
The rosebud...dogwood trees...
But God has already given them to you--
In His beautiful World of Spring!

                    Miriam Janet Dale-Kallas
                    Beech Grove

CHILDREN'S BLESSING

May you experience a feeling of
    belonging so you will be confident.

May you grow to believe in yourself
    and recognize your talents.

May you be loved and encouraged
    yet firmly directed.

May you be praised more and
    punished less.

May someone catch you doing
    something good and
    celebrate with you.

May you learn to reach out and
    touch someone because
    someone reached out and
    touched you.

May you get **all** you need to be
    all you can be.

                        Alice Ann Davis
                        Indianapolis

WAS CHICKEN LITTLE RIGHT?

Who said the sky was falling
Why, Chicken Little did;
But it was just an acorn.
That bonked her on the head.
    MY child, could Chicken Little be right,
        Is the sky falling in your world tonight,
            Or was it just an acorn
                That bonked you on the head,
                    That made you shake with fear,
                        And cry out in your fright,
                            Or run to find mother to make it alright?
My child, in your world are there no goals,
        Nothing is sure and anything goes?
Do men survive to create a superrace,
        Kill little babies,
                And twist love into rape?
Do they sought pleasure without pay,
        Reward without working today?
Do they expect skills without discipline,
        And knowledge without study,
Freedom to take drugs that make the mind like putty?
Yes, my child, Chicken Little was right,
        It's not an acorn,
                But the sky falling in your world tonight!

                        Glenda W. Davis
                        "Little Dove"
                        Waveland

IT'S SUNDAY

It's Sunday
And while God contemplates the rumbles
in his resting bowels
The drake - a gleam in his eye
contemplates the tease twitching tail of his mate.
She - a seeming indifference to her forward looking eye
moves just a mite too quick
for his neck-out waddle.
She preens her feathers by the chicken coop.
He loses interest by the pickup truck
babbles to the adolescent ducks alongside amble in the sun.
She quacks impatiently to herself
a fluster of feathers - preens in a snit now
Settles her sleek shape into indifference
waits for his dandling eye to snag once again
on her tempting tail feathers
catches his eye, hers again indifferently elsewhere
twitches her tail - an accident of movement
and ambles away.
The drake - a gleam in his eye, his neck outstretched
pursues
While God contemplates the rumbles
in his resting bowels
It's Sunday.

Jolon De Leury
Bloomington

SPIDER, SPIDER

Spider, spider on the wall
Aren't you afraid that you might fall
Down from the ceiling to the bed
And then you'd probably hurt your head.

You move so very steathily
Yet graceful every inch
If I could only walk like that
My life would be a cinch.

For you can see in every way
The problems as they come
When you get tired of upside right
You just walk upside down.

A special gift that's given you
And all your spider friends
How very lucky all of you
To walk a path that never ends.

I know you do a lot of good
Eat bugs and flies each day
But even if you didn't
In my home you sure can stay.

And use the talent given you
To spin a web of lace
In a corner on the wall
Your very special place.

Mary V. Deboo
Marion

A WEALTH OF BEAUTY

The beauty of the sunset
Would be no lovelier to behold
If I were clothed in scarlet
And wore bangles of purest gold.

Wealth can never increase
The brilliance of the stars,
Nor can the autumn leaves of gold
Be bought with silver bars.

Carol C. DeSutter
Attica

TIMES OUT

too tired to
and I know
never for a reason
but the moment
almost predicts me
with one yawning glance
about the many
too tired too

Thomas Patrick Doolin
Saint John

FOR THOSE WHO KNOW..?

I seen the war, I died for their want of
peace, but the unknown faces still come
to me, as I lay trying to sleep. The screaming,
crying, with their blood on my hands. will
I ever be able to sleep again...?

When I gave, I gave my all, now I live
behind a forty foot wall, and still the
war goes on in my mind, will it be like
this till the end of my time...?

The screaming, the yelling, the sound of
incoming mortar rounds, the song of a
machine gun, singing its song of death,
the rockets and 105s. It's a wonder, any
of us came home alive.....?

The war is over, or they seem to say, but
I still live in hell at the end of each
day. I close my eyes and try to sleep,
it's back to the jungles, from which I came.
Mortars, machine guns and burning flesh,
"Oh God" I'm back in...Vietnam again....?

Terry Drake
Pendleton

The Poet's Father, Captain Reuben A. Riley

THE POET'S MOTHER, ABOUT 1860

INDIANA AUTUMN

I walked through the woods today.
My dogs were by my side.
I kicked the leaves of gold and brown
And I knew that summer had died.
Gently, swiftly, leaves floated down
And joined their companions on the ground.
Soon they would be covered with a blanket of snow.
And it seemed good to know
That the heavenly Father above
Cares for the woods and the once-green leaves.
It proves over and over his love
For all things of nature and us, His children below.
Even the hounds in their baying
Get the message loud and clear
They seem to be saying "Let's run and enjoy it" –
God's beautiful world.
This splendid time of year!

Patricia D. Drischel
Hagerstown

FULL CIRCLE

Your wedding day has gone, time slipped away before I knew.
Now while quiet and deep in thought, I'll pass this,
daughter, on to you. When I first held you tenderly I
thought that you could never be more beautiful.

Through bicycles and skinned knees, you became more
precious every day. Sports, church and school helped you
grow. There were fears, tears, joy and love along the way.
On your 16th birthday, with eyes aglow and smile so sweet,
I thought: "You'll never be more beautiful."

There were dances,   dating, then falling in love. They're
all a part of God's plan. Before I knew and much too soon
for me, with your Dad you walked down the aisle. Satin
and lace, a sheer veil concealing your face. Flashes of
the past repeated. This must be the day. You'd never be
more beautiful.

Not long ago, I saw through pain, joy and tears, as you
looked upon your own baby girl. Reflecting on days gone
by, I gave a soft sigh. "This is the day." God had made
a full circle in time. As your daughter grows, and the
circle returns to you some day, you'll find it better each
step of the way, and all the more beautiful.

Sharon S. Droll
Russiaville

HALLOWEEN FRIGHT

Halloween is coming, and the witch is on the prowl.
And you hear all kinds of noises, and the goblins start to howl.

The cats are shiny black, and the pumpkins are all lit.
And near the fireplace by your Ma you will sit.

It's really quite a scare, and you have an awful fear.
And isn't Halloween the darkest night of the year.

Liz Dunlap
Indianapolis

MY TREASURE CHEST

Memories are like precious gems,
their value increases with age.
Life has been filled with glorious hymns
that have filled each side of each page.

A friendly word, a kindly deed,
a helping hand in time of need;
so many things along life's way
those little things that fill each day.

Through the years the chest is filled,
the results bring joy untold;
the souvenirs we've put aside
are more precious, by far, than gold.

Down memory lane we pause and reflect
and sort out the trinkets collected;
remembering fondly the time and the place
and many a dear face reflected.

Life rushes on and many thing change
it's the natural flow of life's stream.
But hidden away from public view
is my own personal store house of dreams.

                    Kathleen McCoy Eberly
                    Dyer

JAMES WHITCOMB RILEY: HOOSIER HERO

There's a fellow us Hoosiers is proud to call our own
An' folks that's read 'bout James Whitcomb Riley knows,
Greenfield, Indiana was his home

"Bud" Riley lived afore may of yours' time an' mine
He was born on the eighth of October,
In eighteen forty-nine

I 'spose he growed up like most other boys at that time
Livin' in a log cabin with his family
An' playing at the creek called Brandywine

I sure you've heard of the people he wrote 'bout
Like The Raggedy Man,', an Little Orphant Annie,
An' the gobble-uns 'at git you ef you don't watch out

There was one of his poems titled **Leonainie**
To which was signed Poe's name
'An though the incident was quite a scandal,
It marked the beginning of his fame

Now from town to town and coast to coast
His poems has been read
So let each one of us heed his words
'An toward each other, let something good be said

Marianne Eckhart
Indianapolis

MY SPECIAL MEMORY

Turning back the pages of time
There's always something to remember.
One of my special memories
Is while shopping in December.

Glenna was looking at the dolls,
she had, I don't know how many,
She put one in my arms and said,
"She's crying for her Aunt Ginny."

She knew how to get to me,
And that's one thing for sure.
The next doll that talked to me said,
"Can this girl take me home with her?"

Of course I bought both the dolls.
The next time we went to the store
I had a talk with Glenna,
And the dolls talked to me no more.

Years have passed since that day,
All of her dolls she outgrew,
And with every passing year
There was always something new.

Soon she'll have a real live doll,
Maybe the first of many.
I'd like to hear one more time,
"She's crying for her Aunt Ginny."

Virginia Edington
Bedfore

"KIDS' AND STONES"

Rocks' in my drive-way, I've bought them by the ton,
But my little darlings', gets' rid of them one by one.

They are just kids', and kids' as you know,
See a rock, and they must throw.

They are cute kids', but they're sly as a fox,
But I do wish, they'd quit hitting my mailbox.

They're just tiny, little pebbles, made of lime,
And they're just kids', I know they will surely learn in time.

Some day, they will be all grown and will be gone,
How sad it will be, to have a drive-way full of stone.

Barbara Jean Evans
Shelburn

MY DADDY READ ME RILEY

My Daddy read me Riley in the days gone by,
rhymes to make me giggle and thoughts that made me cry.
He read me Riley cuddled in a great big chair
So I could snuggle closer when I didn't like that bear.

My Daddy read me Riley from his old brown book
But most of it he knew by heart; he didn't always look.
Christmas always came with a Defective Santa Claus
Long before I knew who Santa Claus was.

Daddy read of June-Time, down around the river
And Orphant Annie's stories, but the one that made me shiver
Was the nine green glass-eyed goblins who sent me off to bed
To hide beneath the covers so I wouldn't wake up dead.

My Daddy quoted Riley. His strong calm voice
Taught me God sends rain, so that rain's my choice.
My children hear me crying now, "Get out of my way!
There's time for work, and there's time for play!"

My Dad relived his childhood in a Riley country rhyme
Of parents strict and loving in a slower simpler time.
Throughout his life to show his love he used a Riley line,
Reciting to my Mother from "That Old Sweetheart of Mine".

My memory turns the pages, seeing pictures Dad would show,
But there, with "Old Aunt Mary" and her boys we used to know
With Lizzie Ann and Raggedy Man, a well loved face I see,
And I hear the songs of childhood as my Daddy smiles at me.

Barbara Feigel
Evansville

PRAYER TO ZEPHYR

Pray for the righting of all old wrongs.
Pray, so all wounds hear the healing song.
Pray near the light at the hallway's dark end.
Pray for a life that has just one true friend.

Morning prayer, evening prayer, vesper.
Pray a prayer, pray a prayer to zephyr.

Pray that death's an earned celebration.
Pray for entrance into God's blessed nation.
Pray to soar above the babbling tower.
Don't pray a second when you've an hour.

Morning prayer, evening prayer, vesper.
Pray a prayer, pray a prayer to Zephyr.

Pray on the day that's rife with darkness.
Pray at night when demons are in harness.
Pray for the forgiveness to start anew.
Pray for the many and pray for the few.

Morning prayer, evening prayer, vesper.
Hear my prayer, hear my prayer sweet Zephyr.

Pray for a world unaddicted to killing.
And pray, sweet zephyr, take this prayer
To a God who is ready...a God who is willing.

William W. Ferguson
Indianapolis

TRISTESSEE

I did love you once when
April's greening pregnant with promise
And rainbowed horizons
Held out her arms to us.
But we were weak
Heirs to primal defects
Strongly taloned
And quick to find each other's vulnerability.

I did love you once when
Winter's hand
Steeled with frost and timed with memories
Curled more than once about us.

I weep! I weep!
Sightless yet aimed at stars
And Prometheus-bound
Tortured against black rock.
While waiting the ancient bird
To rise from fertile ashes.

I did love you once, bleeding now
Almost drained against the rack
You forced me to.
But know you then,
I do love you still.

Virginia M. Ferro
Elkhart

SHADOWS

Shadows pass over the moon by night,
Haunting shadows of forlorn trees;
Shadows from the witches' clouds,
Blown by a goblin's breeze.

Spirits come and go to the cornshuck's whisper,
The moon goes by to the banshee's call.
Black cats creep in a vampire's shadow,
The silence is broken by a ghost's footfall.

The dead leaves shiver, the wind is up.
The moon is hidden by a spectre's fingers.
The air is scraped by the wings of a bat -
The shadows grow longer, the night still lingers.

Elizabeth Flood
Greenfield

THE SHADOW STONE

Sioux legend says a sacred stone
hung from Crazy Horse's neck,

and with this amulet
he passed into the spirit side

at will,
and returned at will.

His clothes were pierced by bullets,
but the warrior was untouched.

Sioux legend says a sacred stone
hung from Crazy Horse's neck,

but his people are phantoms,
peddling trinkets and stones.

And if, as legend says,
this world is but a shadow

of the spirit side,
then eternity suffers, too.

Bill Forsythe
Fort Wayne

BUBBLES AND BUTTERFLIES

Bubbles and butterflies,
Blackberry pies,
Babies and puppies,
And old lullabies.

Kittens and cushions,
Vanilla ice cream,
Robins and bird nests,
A mid-summer dream.

Music and books and
Long-legged foals,
Lillies and roses
In white china bowls.

Snowflakes and marigolds,
The sweet mourning dove
Raindrops and songbirds--
All things that I love.

Kathleen Cornelius Fowler
Brookville

A LASTING TRIBUTE TO MY KNIFE

I've hacked, chopped, and sliced,
And I've shaved, peeled and diced,
I've cut flowers and sharpened pencils,
I've scraped paint and cut stencils,
I soon lost my beauty,
From my "overworked" duty,
I've always kept my sharp cutting edge,
I've laid in the drawer and on the counter ledge,
I remember the times you've searched the trash so slimy,
Just because you couldn't find me,
The very worst scare,
Was the time I really was there!
But you cleaned me up with water soapy and warm,
And I continued to faithfully perform,
You've used me many times to prepare one meal,
So no wonder my sharp blade of steel,
Finally got so thin that it vanished away,
Then on that very sad day,
After twenty faithful years,
I brought you to tears,
Because my blade broke in two,
And you even tried super glue,
I've passed every test,
Now, please put me to rest!

"Billie" Francis
Indianapolis

A LIVING TESTAMENT

If you allow God to live within your Heart,
And desire to live righteously,
Quite a difference life would be!
Habit would make you courteous and friendly,
A living testament you would be!

The world would continue as always:
Daily conflicts would still exist,
Temptations won't go away,
Sin would beckon, and often win,
Crime would continue everyday.

But you would know that you
Are responsible for all you do,
You would know that you
Alone, could never make the world anew,
But, you could be an example
For all mankind to see
As a living testament of how the world should be.

Lathan H. Frayser
Indianapolis

BANNERS OF FOREVER

Hail to ol' Gutrie,
great lover of this land.
Tributes to Mister Lennon,
the Imagination man.
Picasso and Miro sparked the colors.
Presidential fathers and courageous mothers
gave us history.
Celestial songs, a Patriot's arms,
bearing smiles of peace and promise.
The Earth and then the Heavens.
A sky encumbered by infinite rainbows.
To be here now is the challenge.
To remember what was is the joy
To wait and embrace tomorrow is brave.
Somewhere, somewhere,
a heart refuses to foil,
and a hero is born.

Gail Galvan
Hammond

THEISTIC EXISTENTIALISM

The is that is is not
The ought I think I sought
"But wait," said God, "For the will be to be
For it is I
Who wrought the thought of ought you think you sought."

Leland Gamson
Marion

FRIENDS

The thoughts that call without a word
The darkest secrets no others have heard
For every hope, for every dream
For every road that has been seen

A fire, a fawn, a standing stone
None other have seen, but we alone
For virtue or vise the paths that run
Toward the moon or to the sun

For this my mind drifts often away
Back on two children of yesterday
I sit and wonder and I think
Of all that we have seen
Of horse shoe ponds and hyacinths
In summers that have been

But, now let us sit beside a fire
And watch our children grow
For they will see a special world
That we will never know

Kelleri Ghent
Garrett

THE PLACE I LEFT BEHIND

I sit by my window
Looking out at the night,
The wind so cool,
The stars so bright.

My imagination soars,
I picture in my mind,
That wonderful place
I left behind.

The time of no care,
Nothing impossible to do,
The oceans I crossed
The mountains too.

The dragons I slayed,
The joust that I won,
The damsel I saved
Just having fun.

I remember the fantasies,
those times way back when,
And I realize that life is
Just as full now as it was back then.

Each time has its joys,
Its sorrow and pain.
If I had a chance,
I'd do it all again.

C. Wayne Gibson, Jr.
Crown Point

A TREE

Some bark is black.
Some bark is gray.
And some of that bark
is all scraped away.

The limbs of the tree
are twisted and bent
And in the trunk
there is a big dent.

The leaves are orange,
red and brown
In the fall
they all fall down.

The trunk stands bare
the limbs, naked and free.
It's a beautiful sight
the big, old tree.

Sonya Nicole Gibson
Crown Point

MOVEMENTS

The yellow gold in my teeth;
Flows through, and to the sea.
My strong heart beats the dirt;
Which moves under me.
Unlike the other heated earth pals;
I know from where I came, and where I go.
Dust around the house, I am soon
With expectations, of my grandchildren to recognize a loon.
Accounting texts are ancestors and unborn;
To the glassed eyes of scorn.
Circle must the earth;
And circle must my constitution.
Open the blind eyes to see.
The greatest mirror of all,
Is the movements of the earth through me.

Glendinning
Indianapolis

MARY CAME ON MONDAYS

Mary came on Mondays
when mamma left all high heeled and silk slipped
Mary came
and knitted orange table mats with kittys smiles and green
      but only along
the border

Mary braided hair
my hair all in rows like woven reeds sticky outy from my head
I watched the Price is Right while Mary braided
fingers poking furious through my heavy mesh and sometimes
      ripping
strands from the white white scalp where mamma's comb had
      missed on
Sunday

my head on Mary's lap
folded rolls of yellowing flesh
tightly tucked in greeny bluish balluppy fabric
a white strap peeking from under one ear
(i tried not to look)
a stocking rip freeing voluminous speckled thigh
Mary was so large i thought she could be god
except she swore and gambled
and damned the white haired lady on the game show who
      couldn't guess the
answer even though the whole audience knew it was two

Mary knitted clucked tongue and teeth and saliva dripped from
      the corners
of her greying mouth
sometimes
and she braided
making me beautiful, like
"an Indian princess" like
"a movie star" like

Belinda Carmichael in the fourth grade who always wore tight
    jeans and full
flowing blouses like Christmas and got the most valentines on
specialfriendday every year

my head in Mary's chest
on rainy days
her giant breasts like hugh thick sacks of milkshake at Dairy
    Queen
falling over my tiny frame
beating down my tiny frame
heavy and solid and making me look at myself in private
    every day but

Sunday

Mary came on Mondays
by Tuesday the braids were gone
wrinkley crinkely sprouts softly scratching my ten year old
    cheeks.

Allison Glock
Bloomington

SULLIVAN COUNTY SUPPER

A farmer a good farmer an old farmer, a good man a family man a good neighbor. His farm, and clapboard house and white, the August sky and blue. Corn yellow with corn yellow.

Sunday and the family comes for supper, comes for family and supper, all floral print women and Sunday talk. Beans in a bowl of cold water. A prayer, then sit and shuffle and pass of food. A long table, men and women, old and young, the dinner and done.

Edward Gohmann
Indianapolis

CIRCLES OF GRAVITY

just as the rain
gently kisses greening earth
gravity drawing circles down
around the whispering rivulets
and into trickling every stream
whence to boiling rivers brown
where every droplet an ocean finds
my thoughts flow back to you

as our gravity tugs within us both
drawing circles with our embraces
we move together in our asymmetries
to find our restless darkened seas
and thinking of you
I smile deeply
from loin to thinning hair
flowering again

John Hayden Greven
Nashville

HITCHHIKER

Dusk, time running out.
In the restless, idle wait
    you spot an office building that
        reflects your presence as
            cars flash by.

On and off, blinding, then blind,
    the image recurs, quite like
        a loop of cinematic tape --
            disarming, hypnotic...

    (Who is that person? Where are they going?
        Is a lover waiting? What promise to be kept?
        What opportunity?)

Suddenly a car horn blares.
You jump, then run to accept an offer.
Just before getting into the car
    You turn, once more, to see your reflection
        in that brilliant, indifferent
            wall of glass, as if
                to seal a memory.

Then gone. Drawn toward a slow rising
    swollen moon, and another phase
        of the monotony of your journey
            out of town.

                    D.L. Grigar
                    Fort Wayne

SPRING BREEZE

She painted her face
blushed and smiled
subservient beauty
raw and naked.

Wrapped in linen
fresh and clean
brushing me lightly
with her eyes.

Soft sweet fragrance
a hint of blossoms
a hint of spring
lulls my senses.

I closed my window
she peacefully slept
until daylight
I let her in again.

Stan Grimes
Logansport

EIGHT MONTHS IN A NONDESCRIPT BAR

(It was like)
Eight months in a nondescript
bar.

A bar - a place
where lights carry out assaults like blitzkriegs
against the eyes, this time with color and
brightness instead of bullets and
bombs. Vision, the victim, becomes
blurred.
- a place where bawdy music
cores into the brain, forcing its way down, ripping
through the neocortex into the lesser mammilian brain.
Intellect diminishes - base instincts
take over.
A nondescript bar.

And I existed here for
eight months.
I found a partner to dance, followed by another
and another
and yet another.
As vision was obscured and intellect absent -
they all appeared attractive, they all looked the same.
They were different (a mystic, a tease, a bitch, a slut.)
They were the same.
Each encounter's end left the same bitterness in my
soul, the bitterness like that found in the backwash
which gathers at the bottom of a bottle of beer.
I was never alone, I was always alone
And with a slight hesitation at the door, I left to be
alone.

Upon exit - I was free.
Under the stars, my soul began
to speak - And like the coyote,
it moaned out its solemn song of yearning.
(They were all the same...)
(They were all the same...)

                    Eric C. Gutjahr
                    Bloomington

THANK YOU, LORD

Dear Lord! Kind Lord!
Gracious Lord! I say,
Thanks for all the lovely things
Thou has sent my way.
For the sunshine after rain,
Rainbow after storm,
Dawn light after darkest night,
Bird song in the morn.
Snowflakes after autumn's glow,
Spring flowers after cold,
Summer days, so bright and fair -
Ere the year grows old.
And for eyes with which to see,
Ears with which to hear,
All the beauties of this land
That I hold so dear.
          Amen

                K. Louise Guyer
                Marion

SIMPLE PLEASURE

My Soul as the river
will flow as free

Slow your mind - to take a drink
then stop - lay by me

Feel my simple pleasure
Hear the gentle tide

A breeze will caress
to strengthen us inside

Days fall behind
to lift us from the past

Finding love along the way
the only love that lasts.

Darrel Hade
Fort Wayne

A PAEAN: RILEY

Riley, poet he
once took up pen,
set down his words,
and shared them. Then,
those who took his thoughts to heart,
emboldened by that leader's start,
have also set down food for minds,
diverse in scope, rhyme of all kinds,
and thought profound, and humorous verse
from poetasters, as I, the curse
of masters of the trade, as he
once was, as set the shape of words,
now used by fools like me, I've heard.
But there are schools that bear his name;
there's hope, and time. Perhaps the same
sort of spark, or love of words, thought from the heart
will dance about in student's dream, then soon to dart
across computers ghastly screen, and might then see the light
of print.
Then satisfied, at last; all smiley, he'd celebrate the
life, of Riley.

H.J. Halterman
Vincennes

USE ME, LORD

Use my lips, Lord
To tell the great story,
Use my hands, Lord
To tell of your glory,
Use my eyes, Lord
To tell of your wonders,
Use my ears, Lord
To listen to blunders,
Use my feet, Lord
To travel the world,
Use my heart, Lord
To hold banners unfurled.

Hazel B. Hansen
Hammond

THIRD SHIFT

Twice as tall as the man,
The punch press stands
And pounds through the night
A steady cadence of punch, two, three, four,
    punch, two, three, four....
As my day ends, a shift begins.
Ten hours (time and a half for overtime)
    on the line.
I hear the beat across the bean field.
Throughout the night for ten hours
    (time and a half for overtime).
I greet the new day, and he, tired,
    grease-flecked,
Climbs into his pickup to go home.

Alice Hartman
Cambridge City

STEVIE IS PKU

Little girl with freckled face.
Hair of red and eyes of green.
No one else can take your place.
Although you're sometimes mean.

Could it be your blood tests,
That make you act just so?
I will always do my best.
To help you, don't you know?

You and your sisters are alike.
In every way but one.
They don't know what it's like.
To get a blood test done.

I stick your fingertip.
The tears fill your eyes.
On a card the blood drips.
It's over, all but the cries.

A genetic disorder.
It's called PKU.
Not hard to care for.
No need to be blue.

With blood tests and diet,
And milk called Phenyl-Free.
A normal healthy child,
My Stevie will be.

Cindy Hartwell
Scipio

INDIANA WEATHER

One day hot and the next day cold-
That's Indiana weather, I've been told!
If our Hoosier weather doesn't suit
Your style-
Just stick around - it'll change in
a while!
So as you watch this week unfold -
Remember, one day hot and the next day cold!

George Haskett
Richmond

SECRET PASSING

A secret passing
of silent oaths-
foresworn to take
my brooding
hide
to a mockingbird's
falling
warble
on the beach of my
backyard.
Enjoyment is a purple
monkey
that swings from limb
to steady
perch-
if I throw
my heart
to flight
I'll know his
soft
fur
well.

Carol L. Hatfield
Indianapolis

MY MOTHER'S HANDS

I looked up from the keyboard and could not understand,
For what I saw before me were my Mother's hands.
These hands that I've been using, while feeling fancy free,
Are not the hands I thought they were, these don't belong to
   me.

I saw these hands some time ago but they were on my Mom,
I don't know how this came to be or where I got them from.
I walked over to the mirror that hangs upon my wall,
And saw to my astonishment, it wasn't me at all!

My Mother's face looked back at me and with a little smile,
Gazed on my look of discontent, of total self-denial.
I could not start to understand how this could all take place
For looking in the mirror at me, I saw my Mother's face.

It seems that age sneaked up on me to claim me as its prize,
It came without a warning and surely in disguise,
It throws my mind into a spin, I readily confess,
To look upon my Mother when I look into the glass.

                          Rosa Hatfield
                          Mentone

AUGUST IS HAVING A PARTY

Dear sweet generous August,
   I love her friendly ways,
She's like a hostess who brings out
   Her very best on well-filled trays.

You've worked and weeded all summer long
   And maybe worried a little, too-
But now, August is having a party
   And she's invited you!

Baskets and pails are filled with good things,
   Tomatoes ripening on the window sill,
And corn on the cob doing something for butter
   That nothing else ever will.

Cucumbers nestled in prickly beds,
   Glistening with morning dew,
Ripening bluberries and green pepper pods-
   I just love August, don't you?

Beautiful, bountiful August
   Don't you love her generous way?
When no one ever need go hungry
   Who planted a seed in May.

That seed you planted so trustingly
   In the cold, unfriendly sod
Has now brought you your just reward-
   Beautiful August, a gift from God.

               C. Betty Risner Hayes
               Rensselaer

A FUNNY BUNNY

My grandaughter bought a hare at the Fair;
A very special kind of a hare.
He is black and white with markings so neat,
A short furry tail and such tiny feet.

He's a cute little species that's called a French Laupe (lop)
His ears don't stand up--they dejectedly flop,
Framing the sides of his face, small and round,
Making him look like a sad Basset hound.

He's frisky and curious as her cat.
He stands on hind legs, gives her plant a "bat",
Knocking off leaves and nibbling away,
'Til she moves the pot and spoils his play.

Then he's off like a feather,
Whirled by the breeze--
If you catch him, just pet him,
But Please--don't squeeze!

Dorothy Gauler Hayman
Highland

"MOODY RIVER"

Moody, muddy river flowing to the sea-

Moody, restless river, often raging, then calm and shining
    free-

I hear your rippling laughter gently nudging against the shore;

The 'Laughing Waters' of long ago and stories of Indian lore-

When the land was young, now your youth is nere' no more.

Moody Mississinewa; lingering memories of fishing trips along
    your banks-

We remember all these times and give you grateful thanks-

Of camping out beneath Indiana's moonlight bright,
The night sounds drifting through the smokey campfires' light.

Cheerful hours, happy times, soothing as the wind-strummed
    chimes-

The sands of the hour glass nearly sifted through as words of
    the poets' rhymes.

Growing older, but ever refreshed with the memory,

Of the moody, muddy Mississinewa, gracefully flowing, ever
    flowing to the sea.

                Carl D. Haynes
                Marion

MAGICAL FANTASY

Magical Fantasy is where we're in a
special loving relationship. You see
jigsaw puzzles of Life and Love fitted so
perfectly together. It's a place where you look
to see a Dream guiding as a beacon. All things
are Fantastic perfectly organized. We are
totally Loved. Sunshine smiles there all
the time. Happy feelings feels us within.
It's a Magical Fantasy. It has a magnetic
pull keeping everything in its own place in,
Life and Love. We know there Who we are,
What we want, how to get it, and Where
we're going. We say, we do, we believe and
it comes true in this Magical Fantasy,
of what we believe life and love to be.
It's a no deal reality a fun and a sad place
to be in a Magical Fantasy, Magical Fantasy.

Barbara Ann (Steele) Hicks
Cambridge City

LOVE GONE SOUR

I feel confined.
The walls are closing in on me --
On us.
I can't breathe.
I'm being suffocated by the closeness --
By you.
I can't handle what you're doing to us --
To me.
This relationship is too much for me
You're too demanding --
Always taking, never asking or giving me anything in return.
I can't live like this --
You're killing me,
As surely as if you'd plunge a knife into my heart.
In a way that is what you're doing.
You **say** you love me --
I know you don't.
I want to be left alone.
I don't want to be confined anymore --
Ever again.

Arlene M. Hittle
Albion

ONE

We're raising you alone
with just your daddy and me
and praying that our love is strong enough
that it's all you'll ever need.

Don't raise him by himself
is all we ever hear;
'You'll be wanting to have
another one in just another year.'

It's just that in these times
things are rough enough
We don't want you to ever do without
Any of the important "stuff".

You'll always have an abundance
of love and understanding
And hopefully you'll also learn
of responsibility and sharing.

We hope that as you grow older
You'll understand our reasons;
It's merely that you are number ONE!
To us during every season.

Rena E. Holcomb
Hagerstown

GOD CARES FOR ALL

Out under the canopy of heaven -
   I see the beautiful skies
God in the wonder of creation
   Has given love for the living our lives.

Go tell the world how I love them
   Show people the way to take
How God in great glory and splendor
   Has given His love for our sake.

'Tis not the land that He loves
   'Tis not the splendor He made
It is rather the soul within us
   That brings God cause to give aid.

O happy ones and holy
   O joy beyond compare
How great and faithful God is
   To lift us above all care.

            L. George Hostetter
            Fairmount

MY DREAM

Oh, if life were but a dream,
How wonderful it'd be.
When things are bad-I'd just wake up,
To put my mind at ease.

No worries, no troubles, no need to want,
Everyone would have everything they need.
Oh, if life were like my dream,
What a happy life we'd lead.

No need to be angry,
Only Love never Hate.
Life would have a plan,
Never left to fate.

Oh, if life were like a dream,
So many hopes and prayers it'd fill.
But I'll patiently wait for my dream to come true,
Because one day I know that it will.

Amy Hougland
Kokomo

FORGOTTEN TIMES

The war is over and we are free: Then why is there
men still missing that no one has seen. Some have deserted
some are dead but there is still some alive and missing
in Vietnam.

People have searched high they have searched low they
asked questions but no one knows about the men dead and
buried in Vietnam. Family and friends of these men try
to make it on their own and hope some day they will come
home.

Della Howe
Bloomington

PART OF ME FOUND

Why should I fight tears from my eyes;
doesn't life supply extremes.
There are times to laugh and times to cry.
Why are my tears so shy?
When I break inside or feel sad
the urge to express myself and weep never falls deep.
I have been made tough by broken hearts in the past.
I have walls that stand tall between the parts of me
that I once knew well.
These are places where deep feelings lie
unused untouched they haven't so much as seen light
because it's a dark place in my heart
that keeps them apart from me.
But I found them and I shook them loose
I put them to use and I made them
work for me, work with me
and assume their place in my heart.
It's a reflective place in my soul
that gives me perspective
and makes me a whole human being.
Again my tears have become part of me.

Edward G. Howe
Crown Point

FOR MY SISTER, WHO WANTS A CHILD

By the stream
white cows lay against each other
like smooth river stones
bleaching in the sun,
their mouths leaking
saliva onto the grass
in slow strands of wet cotton.

One, on her side
blasts deep animal groans.
The pain of life inside her turns
violently against the belly
wanting air.

Five heavy birds
float above, angling
their thick wings
to slice cleanly through
the heat of August.

And I wait
on the porch.
I watch (arms folded
around my empty middle)
as if waiting,
as if watching were enough.

Christina Hubble
Bloomington

THE BOOKWORM

He's ne'er alone, who loves his books,
    They're friends abiding, true,
Always they're near, to comfort and cheer,
    When the weary day is through.

Adventure is his, and philosophy,
    And he loses himself in dreams,
Windmills he'll slay, or Tecumseh be,
    Or party to Shakespeare's schemes.

Another's thoughts on paper,
    His soul revealed, bared,
Their being attuned together,
    With dreams forever shared.

Yes! the pleasantest way to end the day,
    If companions, rare, delight,
Is an easy chair, an apple or pear,
    And a book by the firelight.

                    Leafy Hudson
                    Mentone

INDIANA PICNIC

Mabel, Mabel, set the table!
Yates, Yates, get out the plates!
Lee, Lee, sweeten the tea!
Sam, Sam, slice the ham!
Fred, Fred, unwrap the bread!
Rickles, Rickles, open the pickles!
Dicken, Dicken, set out the chicken!
Bruce, Bruce, pour the juice!
Newt, Newt, get out the fruit!
Teddy, Teddy, the beans are ready!
Knips, Knips, open the chips!
Meigs, Meigs, uncover the eggs!
Jake, Jake, cut the cake!
Helen, Helen, start a yellin'!
Yell as loud as you are able,
Get 'em here and down at the table!
Ace, Ace, say the grace!
All right now, put on a grin,
Pass them vittles and all dig in!
Somebody must have been real flustered--
Somebody sure forgot the mustard!
Oh, well!

Dorothy L. Hunt
Indianapolis

RETROAPECTION

When I look back across my span of life
The times of early youth come into view;
My memories are strangely free of strife
As I recall the many joys I knew.
The carefree days I followed every whim
That lured me down cool, shady country ways,
The gravel pit where first I learned to swim,
Green meadows where glum cattle slowly graze;
Ice-skating on a frozen winter pond,
A sleigh ride through a snowy afternoon,
Deep friendships welded with a solemn bond,
The golden days that faded all too soon.
In reveries that never cease to thrill,
Those happy moments linger with me still.

Charles P. Isley
Merrillville

SWEET BRANDYWINE!

Let's drift back to the 'Olden Days'
The pace 'twar slow, the livin' fine -
Kick off yer shoes, roll up yer pants
Wiggle yer toes in Brandywine!

Pickin' wild berries in the bresh
In itchy, dirty, torn ol' clothes -
Gnats, 'skeeters, crawlin up yer legs
The smell o' dust, ticklin' yer nose!

The bobbin' cork's atwitchin' hard
Fightin' mad, 'twar thet ol' catfish -
Mama fried 'em, juicy n' sweet
My, warn't thet a lip smackin' dish!

O'er the Old Covered Bridge, we'd run
Skim stones 'crost the clear, ripplin' stream -
Take a dip near the noisy Dam
Lie down to rest - dream on, sweet dream!

Stumblin' round in thick bramble stand
Scratches 'long our hot, sweaty face -
Thorns snagged in our arms, legs and tush
Not sure we'd E'ER leave thet dern place!

Such joys we had in youngster ways
Fishin', swimmin', life 'twar sublime -
Songs n' laughter, soft carefree days
All up n' down Sweet Brandywine!

RoseMarie Jackson
Knightstown

RAGGEDY MAN

He huddles in deserted doorways
doused in dust and cringed by cold,
as ageless now as on that day
when I was eight years old.
The rank perfume of sour mash
pervaded his cement domain
and anyone with eyes could see
he'd won the losing game:
The wrinkled skin grimed grey by dirt,
the stubbled chin, the yellowed teeth,
a tattered collar bunched below
and, God knows, underneath....

But to a child, here was a man
of ancient mysteries, and wise
with all the knowledge of the world
caught in his squinty eyes.
'Tell me a truth, old man,' I begged,
'where happiness can best be found
and when the butterfly will sing
and why a coin is round.'
He wiped a fist across his mouth
and raised his nodding, hair-wisped head:
'There are no shadows on the sun,'
was all he ever said....

Carole A. Jenet
Kokomo

GRANDMA'S LEGACY

On her knees
she clawed through dirt and decay
to plant her daffodils

She moistened their roots
with gentle tears of anguish
fearing the ugly amber flood
would wash them away

Every year she planted them
Every year they bloomed

She grew older and smaller
A scream rose from her soul
and tried to break through her eyes

The last spring there were no daffodils
There were no tears

The scream is growing inside me

Linda Ward Johnson
Marion

INDIANA

"I am an American... Every drop of blood in me holds a heritage of patriotism.... I am proud of my Past."
                              (Elias Lieberman)

Salute the men who made our Hoosier state;
Salute the brains, the brawn
    that helped to make her great.
Recall to mind her heroes.
    great and small
    that built a state
    whose citizens stand tall.

Mark well the ones who wrote, who fought,
    who led,
Take off your hat, as well,
    to those who bled
    that freedom's flag might wave.

Pray for the strength and courage
    that they gave to carve a state
    from out a virgin soil,
And note that this was done by sweat and toil.
And, as you count the blessings
    that they gave,
Remember well that these
    we cannot save
Unless we, too, reach high
    to grasp the stars.
God's gifts that were their own
Can still be ours.

                    Ruby A. Jones
                    Muncie

SONNET

When I last stopped at Whitcomb Riley's grave,
The ultimate rumble of the Crown Hill
Chapel's throbbing chimes signified no ill
Greater than another withered soul's brave
Passage from the dank reliquary's nave
To the perfect redemption of the till
Below. So I admired the codicil
Elucidation this simple tomb gave
My skeptic spirit, the staid Ionic
Order in fair complicity with the
Sybaritic scene surrounding me. Yet,
I somehow feel the purer aesthetic
Of that dim evening was the play of three
Children on the banks that hold the poet.

Chris Katsaropoulos
Indianapolis

POEM TO J.W.R.

Mayapples in season,
I ran with my cousin,
Shelled corn in the crib,
Raced bikes for no reason.

Mrs. Claypole watched us,
Next door, from her window.
"Try not to worry her,
...was a stroke," Mom told us.

We swam in the green creek,
Getting out with leeches,
Waded in the sheep dip,
Mixed chick babes with ducklings.

"Your kids are on the roof,"
"They're heading for the lake,"
"Striking matches on the walk!"
"Maude's had a stroke," Mom said.

"The goblin'll git cha."
Mom'd read aloud at night.
"Read us more," cousin said,
Pushing back our bedtime.

Mayapples in season,
Meant time to hunt mushrooms,
Shoot arrows with cousin,
Race bikes for no reason.

                    Ann Kautzmann
                    Cynthiana

"MAGIC" SNOW

Remember when we liked it well
Upon the days that new snow fell.

The world was quiet as a prayer
Dressed in its pure, white snowy layer,

And you and I were snug inside
Thinking how our sleds would slide.

Later the snow was marred with traces
Of all our steps to sliding places;

And we'd stay outside in the cold
Far too long and Mom would scold;

For Mother never seemed to know
The "magic" quality of snow;

And yet we somehow found a way
To tuck that magic snow away

Within our hearts where yet today
We still run through the flakes and play.

I'm no longer glad to see snow fall--
It's so much trouble for one and all,

But the snow that fell in those days past
Will be a pleasure to the last.

Betty L. Killebrew
Clinton

BENEATH THE GOLDEN MOON

Beneath the golden moon I see
Oak and Elm and Walnut trees,
Swaying in the gentle breeze
To the crickets symphony.

Reflections of a graceful deer
Shines on the water crystal clear,
Bathed in the light from the golden beams
She stands beside the running stream.

Golden wheat and ripened corn
Glistens with dew in the early morn,
Shimmer and sway beneath the light
Like soldiers marching in the night.

Beneath the golden moon I see
Everything that God gave me,
Beauty framed in a golden ray
That's often missed throughout the day.

Loretta Kinley
Lafontaine

DAY AT THE BEACH

The day was oh, so beautiful.
The sand was oh, so white.
The water beckoned, please come in,
It was a gorgeous sight.
We gathered bathing suits and towels,
We packed a picnic lunch
Then set off for the beach that day,
We were an eager bunch.
The sun felt warm and cozy.
The water was just right.
We sat around, then swam a bit
As long as it was light.
Then it was time to leave behind
The wonders of the day,
And suddenly all turned to work
What just before was play.
We grumbled as we gathered towels,
Picked up picnic debris.
We trudged our way back to the car
A sorry sight to see.
But 'ere another week goes by
We'll start out fresh once more
For only happy memories stay--
Sad ones are such a bore!

Frances N. Kohn
MIchigan City

APRON STRINGS

Cutting is an art
best mastered by sons,
honed by fathers, who know
the fastest way through a knot,
a slash, the quick skill of slicing
flesh from a fish, severing scales
to fall like buttons
from a worn-out shirt.
Daughters, on the other hand,
learn from their mothers
the art of tying, of weaving
one thread to another.

"Watch me," say the fathers,
as they hold razors
to their lathered faces.
But mothers say to daughters,
"take my hand."
When a thread is cut, they learn
to slide another
through the needle's eye.

While sons may inherit
their fathers' watches,
every daughter carries
the bones of her mother's fingers,
tangled in her apron pocket,
lumpy as clothespins, but still
nimble enough to fasten
new lives onto the line.

              Barbara Koons
              Indianapolis

NOTHING'S HALFWAY

The sun never stops in the middle of the sky;
A bird never glides when learning to fly.
A leaf never falls halfway from the tree;
Nothing's halfway, can't you see?
The war is not over if only one side goes home;
If the keystone should fall so does the whole dome.
A revolution won't end with the raising of a single hand;
Nothing's halfway, can't you understand?
Rain falls without a choice;
There is no one deaf to a single voice.
Peace does not stand for just one dove;
Nothing's halfway, especially love.

Patrick A. X. Koontz
Vincennes

HIS STONE

The stone felt cool. I rubbed my hands
along its rigid, frigid breast
and felt how smooth, except the grooves
whose tracings told the tale of death
and how the one who lay there found his rest.

Hero maybe, maybe not. Who knows and who now cares
for surely those who loved him are now with him.
Whatever praise or punishment he now receives
I do not know, and only those cold markings bore
the memories of those who grieved.

I laid my head against the stone
and let the cool caress my brow
and try to somehow reach that time when he
once walked as living flesh and bone
and no one had yet thought of me.

A kindred bond reached through the graves
His conventional, once honored, once floral wreathed
And mine yet recognized. No one yet had carved my name.
But the lead that killed at Bunker hill
At Mai Lei killed the same.
And his stone stood forgotten.
And mine as yet unseen.

Ross A. Lakes
Bluffton

VILLAGE RAILROAD

In lingering curve it lies across the town,
Then levels off as if in glad goodbye
To guarded crossings, flicker lights, and down
South to the bigger towns, straight as a die.
The village folk are glad to see a train,
Admiring hosts to such impatient guest.
They like its hustling, clamorous refrain,
The pent-up diesels, --wheels that seldom rest.
Although, for some who cannot jaunt away,
Those parting blasts enhance a loneliness
Not known to those who've never had to stay
Forever settled. Yet these folk progress:
Their wares are taken swiftly down a line
That knows the sea, the plain, the mountain pine...

                    Harlan J. Leach
                    Marion

FRUITFUL SILENCE

From years of tears
The grief in my soul
Would pour forth on paper
As a wound gushes blood.
Poetry out of pain.

In time the flow was staunched
And the healing process begun.
Step by step the therapy went on,
Rehabilitation of a crippled spirit.

My pen lay silent during that time
My heart too weak for expression.
But that One who loved me as I was
And sees me as I am to be
Has called me sufficiently healed to speak.

From life now within me
The gratitude in my soul
Pours forth on paper
As life-giving rain showers the ground.
Poetry from thanksgiving.

                    Evelyn L. Lees
                    Noblesville

BALCONY BATHING BEAUTIES

Our two-story limestone home
with eleven rooms has a leaded glass
picture window that dances prisms
across the living room when the sun
shines through it, and a winding staircase
with a sky light above it.
A balcony, the width of the house, is a beach
for my sister and me.

We lie on Grandma's handmade quilt
spread on the yellow-tiled floor, and it soaks
up the sunscreen slathered on our sweaty bodies.
When we can stand the heat no longer,
we run into the house and jump into the shower
with our swimming suits on.
Drenched, we run back to the quilt and throw
ourselves down to be baked like pattycakes.

We spend free time sunning on the balcony
where we're safe from the googly eyes
of the neighborhood boys.
We sun and bathe, bathe and sun,
and cover ourselves with tanning and body
lotions until we're sleek and brown
like water dogs.

                              Janet Leonard
                              Taswell

THE GRAY HOUSE

The house was gray
    was gray with years
It begot his hopes;
    it begot his fears.

And now the man
    the man became
A carbon copy
    of his own domain.

Pat Levy
Ft. Wayne

SCARS ARE BURNING

Scars are burning
Wounds look healed
Deep within our hearts they're sealed.
Probing rays of holy light
Illumining darkness beyond our sight;
Untangling masses deep within,
Straightening heart-strings
Bent by sin.
Scars are burning
Wounds look healed
The Holy Spirit works
Concealed.

Gail Littell
Campbellsburg

ICE AGE

Snow bright night,
Frozen deer tracks cross my path.
Squeaking footsteps pierce the silence,
Echoing desolation.
Vague remembrance of summer's sunshine
Spurs the spirit to persevere
Until the earth warms green and birds return.

Carol Jean Locke
Westfield

THE BROKEN KEY

I offered to you my heart, my soul
For these, you said, you had little need
For many a suitor wanted you
Quite naturally, you were most pleased.

So many keys seem to fit your heart
"Dear me, what's the matter with mine?"
Why! It's bent and it's bruised, yes broken
To mend it would take much precious time!

On I must go in quiet despair,
Always loving and missing you so
With my key broken beyond repair
Without choice, having to let you go.

Shirley Longnecker
Cambridge City

GLAD I'M A HOOSIER

I'm sa glad thet I'm a Hoosier,
And kin live in Hoosierland
Ta see the beauties God has made
Fur us on ever' hand.
When I look at the purty trees
An' hear the birdies sing,
Er see the flowers bloom sa brite
And purty ever' spring,
I feel like God was parshull to
Us Hoosier folks, somehow,
'Cause He gave us a speshull state----
The best one, I'll allow.
'Tain't hard ta see why Hoosiers is
Sa lucky ever' way,
'Cause Indiana's best of all
The states ther is, I'd say,
An' I'm shore glad that I kin be
A Hoosier, thru and thru;
I'm lucky thet I got ta be
A Hoosier-borned. Ain't you?

                    Jeanne Losey
                    Shelbyville

ONCE A TRAVELER

Once a traveler set out on his way
Led by his dreams and desires
Past houses and farms and hay-filled barns
And little churches with white painted spires.

Then that day came when the path he crossed
Of the woman who would be his wife
She stole his heart from his sleeve,
His plans to leave and his love for the rest of his life.

Now they travel as one down that old dusty trail
Full of ruts and detours galore
But he's happier by far with her by his side
Than he's ever been before.

So he's writing this tale in hopes to convey
This message so clear and so true
If you counted his blessings it'd be easy to see
At the top of the list would be you.

                    Ollin O. Lotten
                    Marion

PEACE LIKE MINE

There is no peace like mine
I glide silently on quiet rivers,
watching no shore for detail
I see no man who threatens me,
no woman pressing for my time
I feel no urgent call to move
for someone else,
no demand for thoughts
I sense activity nearby
but pass it calmly
I let the world go on
doing its business without me

Here on quiet rivers
I find my time for dreaming
I fill my heart with only my desires
I feel only my own breezes,
and taste only my own life.
There is no peace like mine

John C. MacLeod
Bloomington

TO LIVE WITHOUT INDEPENDENCE
IS TO DIE WITHOUT DEATH

My parents planted a seed, the rows
sown with Riley, Stevenson and Field. My
father wrote poems for me to recite. Too
young to know what was filling my psyche's
storehouse, I heard Dreiser, Gene Stratton
Porter and Lew Wallace mentioned around
the house as if they were acquaintances.
To be a Hoosier was the ultimate pride and
to be a **Hoosier Writer** was the ultimate
immortality.

By age 45, the seed of Hoosier writers
kept sprouting; it got to be like honeysuckle,
it took root, it began to cover my mental
embankments; it began to strangle.

Poetry became a catalyst to reveal in
print the unacceptable: to raise hell in a
formalized way that society will tolerate;
to come to terms with all the untouchables
long buried under the security blanket of the
old ways--the comforting but mentally lethal
ways.

Intellectual freedom, as well as all other
freedoms, demands responsibility. What I
have discovered about myself, through poetry,
allows me to share the daring and the
rewards of my experience with other poets,
writers, and even mental patients. That is
why I am a **Hoosier Writer**!

Normajean MacLeod
Bloomington

TENEMENT

The woman sits on the step
    with her dirty face--
Watching me walk--I slow--
    conscious of her, I pace.

I study her eyes for secrets kept.
See nothing. Be nothing. Let the spoiled dishes
    pile to the sky. Let the cancerous cat purr low,
    lose interest in fish bones and feline wishes.

I look at the stoop where bums have slept.
Her foot twists on the spot, engraving the ground
    with a gravely signature. She does not know
    that the blood behind my eyes begins to pound,

or that I will dream of her tonight.

                        Timothy Macy
                        Muncie

INDIAN MAIDEN ON THE BANKS
OF THE IROQUOIS RIVER

The Indian maiden washed her hair near the bubbling rapids
In the sparkling waters of the Iroquois River.
The fragrance of pine drifted in the air, as she bathed in the
    waters
In the sun bronzed skin God gave her.
As she shakes her head; the warm breezes of the air
Caress and dry her long dark-flowing hair.
She washes her clothes on the flat rocks by the river's edge
On a near prairie she pitches tent and makes her bed.
She sleeps under the moon and stars so bright,
Dreaming, wondering what may come in the future's light?
But, could she see in the future what was near;
The old iron bridge, the city of Rensselaer?
Could she forsee her people gone from the beautiful water
    fall?
Not knowing where they went, not knowing at all.
Sprinkled on the winds, blown across the nation
She would wonder at this incredible revelation.
Oh yes; the Indian maiden washed her clothes near the bub-
    bling rapids,
In the sparkling waters of the Iroquois River.
And the fragrance of pine drifted in the air, as she bathed
In the waters, in the sunbronzed skin God gave her.

                            Anna Marlin
                            Rensselaer

MENDING LIST

Hem that ragged horizon
Basted fluffy clouds in place
Fashion tucks across the field
Along the fence row gather lace
Cut elbow patches for the oaks
Darn the holes worn in the hill
Run ribbon through the apple trees
Sew the brook an extra frill

                              Jane Wilson Maskel
                              Kokomo

SEEN BUT NOT HEARD

Before the war parents shouted,
"Children should be seen
But not heard,"
So he quietly played alone.

During the war protesters shouted,
"Soldiers should be seen
But not heard,"
So he quietly fought alone.

After the war employers shouted,
"Vietnam Vets should be seen
But not heard,"
So he quietly worked alone.

After his death mourners whispered,
"Actions speak louder
Than words,"
And he quietly died unheard.

Robin M. Mathy
Bloomington

OLD BRANDYWINE

It was very warm and muggy that September afternoon
as I sat along "old brandywine" and thought, Autumn
would be here soon.
Then I suddenly heard gleeful laughter of prankish
boys in fun, even saw their skinny bodies glistening
in the sun.
Mr. Riley"'s "Old Swimmin Hole" was suddenly alive
again filled to over-flowing with splashing
water, fun, and grins.
But as I sat there with this vision a withered
leaf came floating down and the only things
that seemed alive were me and this old stream
rippling along in silent sound.
How sad it is to say that the future of this
stream can only be a flowing force for fallen
leaves and a place for dreaming dreams.

Barb Maxwell
Greenfield

GOD'S SEASONS OF THE WORLD

When the wind is blowing strong,
And the rains come pelting down,
Who brings us all this water,
To thirsty lands and trees?

When the snow takes its turn,
And piles high in mounds around,
Who is responsible for such enormous beauty,
Gathered all around the towns?

Then spring peeps through the grounds,
And grows and grows and grows,
With plants and flowers and leaves and such,
From the soil of fertile grounds.

Comes fall when all will disappear,
And all will look so bare,
To remind us of the One that is,
The Master of seasons gone by.

Can you remember whence all this has started,
Or whence it has ended, too,
Well let me tell you or can you guess,
It's God's homeland made for you.

What a blessing, what a joy,
To hear the wind again,
From some, unseen Force,
Who created the seasons of the world.

Ann M. Mayes
New Whiteland

CORNER REVERIR

Hurrying footsteps on a busy thoroughfare:
where are they going in a never-ending parade?

Down the street come dainty high-heeled slippers.
At a flower shop they stop and then begin again.

Quiet steps are replaced by firm ones of neat oxfords.
They, too, stop at the shop as homeward they wend the way.

Weary plodding steps, lagging steps
Too tired to stop for beauty pass upon the corner.

Dusk falls, shops close,
The corner is deserted, silence.

With sudden noise pelting footsteps round the corner
They slacken, slaken, stop beneath a silver moon.

Patent shod feet move as if afraid of lingering.
At sudden noise they take to flight while Lady Moon keeps
    silent watch.

Mismated, broken shoes, stumbling footsteps toward a door-
    way
Where they will remain the night for rest.

Footsteps, footsteps of humanity passing upon the corner;
Passing in day, passing at night.

                            Fances Helmerick Mc Bride
                            Crown Point

LIFE

Life is what you make it
You have often heard it said
Be a success or be a failure
Lag behind or forge ahead.

When life's problems come upon you
Don't let trouble get you down
Grit your teeth and face the future
Wear a smile and not a frown.

Life is not a bed of roses
There must be some rough spots too
So if you look upon the bright side
You can make your dreams come true.

                    Bernice McGriff
                    Marion

A POET

Most Poets are very shy, can't speak aloud,
always in the background, but very proud.
With pen in hand, writing what they see,
expressing nature how beautiful it can be.
A time when writing is very very sad,
A child is abused, A small little lad.
The elderly being treated with disrespect,
hoping some one will read with interest to reject,
what goes on in our world today,
erase the fear give back love to stay.
A poet shares his thoughts through verse or rhyme
with compassion and love in every line.

                              Christol Mc Kee
                              Richmond

SITTING IN THE PARK

...I yearn to cry
   and cry
until the birds halt their songs
and listen with cocked heads
   in thronged stillness
     --and understand.
Instead, I crumble and scatter
the remnants of my bread
    --and life,
soothing my wounds,
  confessing wrongs,
    choosing progress
      through winged demands.

Shirley Vogler Meister
Indianapolis

THE LITTLE RED SCHOOL HOUSE

Today I passed the little red school house
It seemed such a joy to me
Restored just like the school house
It was the one I cherished in memory

For then it didn't hurt to walk a mile or two
To get an education
It was up to you to learn
As you dreamed of graduation

The dipper and the water bucket
Was in reach of every girl and boy
To dip into that bucket
To the thirsty was a joy

The little red school house was heated
By a large pot bellied stove
No matter where we were seated
We wished to be nearer the stove

Little Red school now rests on a grassy knoll
For the present generation
Recalls the joys of girls and boys
Held by all now in veneration

                    Nellie Merrill
                    Hammond

GRANDMA'S QUILT

A thousand moons have cast their light
Across the creamy, tufted waves
Of candlewick and careful stitch,
Recalling long forgotten days.

Once virgin white to welcome love
Placed gently on her wedding bed;
It captured dreams and vesseled tears
Helped ease the morning tasks ahead.

Her newborn babe, the frightened child,
A neighbor rescued from the cold--
All found a sleepy welcome there
Beneath its warm inviting folds.

A wreath of comfort in old age;
Her shroud for death in darkened room
Then carefully placed upon a shelf
With petals sweet from summer's bloom.

So many lives have touched this cloth;
A family chronicle in thread
Passed down to me as grandma wished,
This cherished quilt adorns my bed.

Joan Potter Messing
Otterbein

A PAPER DOLL

Pretty and perfect and so neatly dressed,
a wardrobe of clothes, she must look her best.
Picked up and played with, and then laid aside,
an image on paper with features applied.

A paper doll is not real.

A party, a date, now what must she wear,
the latest in fashion will attract many stares.
A painted image is what she reflects,
no character flaws to establish defect.

A paper doll's thoughts are concealed.

Controlled by others whenever they choose,
no heart to be broken, nothing to lose.
A game of pretend that lasts for awhile,
then placed in a box along with her smile.

A paper doll cannot feel.

Cindy Michael
Bloomington

THE OLD FARM HOUSE

(a true story)

There is an old farm house in Indiana
That's changed quite a bit from days of yore.
But one thing still remains the same,
there's never been a lock on the old back door.

My sister lived in this quaint old place;
her two girls went to sleep without a fear.
While all was dark and silent 'round the house,
anyone could have made an entrance at the rear.

In time three sturdy little boys joined the gals.
Now five children with Mother and Daddy farmed the farm.
Tho' they might secure windows against rain and snow,
the back door remained unlocked, without a bit of harm.

But bad times came upon this family;
things did not go well.
But thru it all, one thing remained,
the back door never needed a bell.

For several years only two boys were there.
This made the old house very still.
And tho' they both would leave sometimes,
anyone could enter by the back at will.

Now, there's only one son left to care for this old home,
but he's a trucker and drives this country o'er.
So, the old house just takes care of itself,
and there's still no lock on the old back door.

Stanford Ned Miller
New Castle

LET YOURSELF GO

When you are at the bottom of the rope
You have no place to turn to
Or a place to go
You believe your life is through
There is nothing new
You do not know what to do
Always remember
Your dreams will help you
To turn your life around
As you cross a path of uncertainty
You do not know who to believe
Or what is coming down
Your dreams are your goals
There is someone who can help you
To make your dreams come true
The man in the sky knows
Shoot the bow and arrow
Let yourself go

Diane Marie Mirich
Merrillville

OUR LITTLE TOWN

Our little town isn't nestled in the rockies, or cuddled on the
sands of the sea,
Our little town is in central Indiana, and its houses and its
people suit me.

We have the Joneses and Tydalls and the Grants, we have
the poor and that's me,
Our little town is a quaint little town, t'was the home of the
Fiddler's three.

We have two banks and loan companies three, without them
just where would we be?
We would burn cobs in the old cook stove, and wish for vaca-
tions by the sea.

We have it in the bag with K C L, we're packed secure by I P C,
We never were framed by P P G, and we don't get a shock from
G.E.

Our little town is on the banks of big blue, where the bears of
Blue river might be,
We have them down town on the public square, where all of
our friends can see.

Our little town is a quaint little town, not noted for a poet or
a tree,
Our little town is the home of Sandy Allen, that makes us fa-
mous you see!

Our little town is a great little town, won't you share this en-
thusiasm with me?
Our little town here in central Indiana called Shelbyville
IN-DI-AN-EE!!

                              Neoma Monroe
                              Shelbyville

WARNING

Path of Righteousness
Oh narrow road.
Posted with signs
Conflicting
Contradicting,
Confusing.
The straight and narrow
Isn't straight.
There are perilous twists (of fate)
And numerous exits (off)
Beware Travelers.

Neta Morefield
Crown Point

JAMES WHITCOMB RILEY
Age twenty-two

THE POET IN 1896

HAIKU WEST

The rotting pumpkin
Lying still in the garden
Forgotten by all

Forests hold secrets
Known by many a person
Understood by few

Bethany C. Morgan
Bristol

MEMORIAL DAY PRAYER FOR THE POPPIES

Where cannons boomed
skulls rolled and flew.
The Holy Spirit dead.
The little children soon abed,
the bloodshed soon forgotten
except for this one day a year
when some eat beef and chicken.

The army's dear where marching
    bands
greet waiting hands. They want--
Soon! Soon! -- three billion bucks
    a day.
The military bands will stay.

"Soon! Soon!" the poppies seem to say,
as heads nod in the wind,
"All nuclear warheads doomed."
In Flanders Fields the poppies bloom
where there is only standing room.

Barbara Mosemann
Elkhart

BILL WARD

He, Too,
was
too new
to know
how it feels
not
to be free.

I mean
it must take some
getting used to:
this not belonging.

I don't know:
Is there a book
I could read
on being unwanted?

not fitting in

stinking with no smell

(just **look** like you stink)

White folks can be terrible mean
to their own kind
sometime...

treat them like
they was niggers.

perhaps that's what made him
want to leave this place...

ain't no white man in his right mind
want to be no nigger....

Frank Motley
Bloomington

SPIRALING

The spiral tightens, lifts us -- we go round
the climbing circle formed of years by days,
with special days defining years in ways
that mark them off, and in the years are found
our reaching and our growing. We find too
we watch the years pass inexorably,
looking up and down and back and forth, and see
high-lighted things we could and could not do,
too late the things we did and did not know.
Now as the spiral turns, our longer view
reflects all that we hoped, and what came true
of where we were and where we hoped to go.
And thus we learn time spirals: every year
goes higher, growing shorter and more dear.

Fleta P. Newlin
Kokomo

THE VISIT

We went to visit Aunt Stella.
She was 100 years old today
and still lives in the country,
close to the creek...won't own
a telephone. Pawpaw pie, large
brown eggs, and crabapple jelly
sent us to her.

We talked of politics and
religion without debate, until
she asked, "What's folks gonna
do with sorrows, if they ain't
never been saved?" Studying her
lack of needs we left, feeling
a "back then" rightness.

Janet Nybakke
Crawfordsville

REFLECTIONS

Time moves on
unfaltering
unaware of my heart's pain

Time remains
unchanging
remiss of my life's change

Love slips past
fleetingly
elusive butterfly

Love is so
selective
oh, to qualify!

Ruth Ann Osborn
Ft. Wayne

THE SUMMER OF '67

Remember the summer of '67
    I was five and you were ten
maybe eleven.
    The days were full of
heaven's bliss.
    Oh, how those days are
sorely missed.
    Days full of dreams, songs,
and hope.
    We did not know of fatal screams,
cries of hunger, or crack to smoke.
    to be five, ten, or eleven......
Just to relive the summer of '67

                    Gabrielle Penermon
                    Indianapolis

IN APRIL

Behind the lightgrey clouds
it's lying in wait
to jump at us unexpectedly,
spring,
the capricious dancer
that unleashes annoying shackles
which winter imposed on us.

It doesn't commit itself
to a fixed time and day,
reveals neither origin nor arrival,
keeps its secret, makes promises
which are not always kept.

We trust and distrust it,
want to believe yet have to doubt,
grope in the dark amidst bursting light.

Carol Petersen
Valparaiso

HORSE SHOE LAKE, 1986

We went to the lake the other day my friend and I.
We threw rocks in the water and watched the geese fly.
We walked hand in hand along a rocky path
We met a man who said howdy and then he tipped his hat.
People sat along the fishing banks
Not really giving a hoot
Catching perch, catfish, and frogs and even sometimes a boot.
Bar-B-Q smoke raced through the air
The scent enticed the nose
Someone's meat has caught on fire
Quick bring a water hose.
Children running here and there playing tag at best
Babies sleep on blankets and in buggies
Trying to get their rest.
The old folks sat in lounge chairs telling a tale or two
We stopped and listened while each joined in with laughter from
    the group.
Hand in hand, heart in heart we continued on our way
The sunshine bright, no rain in sight, oh, what a perfect day.
As the day comes to an end, we begin to pack our gear
Not really wanting the day to begin and now the end's so near.
We sat by the water's edge side by side
Holding each other's hands
Watching the setting of the sun while making tomorrow's plans.
Wondering where did the day go as the darkness set in
A full moon appear that only lovers know
Sat me and my friend.

Carolyn Peterson
Hammond

HEPBURNESQUE

Powder puffed fine gal,
Sweet Givenchy go go vamp,
Revlon bop princess!

Pop punk-rock divine,
Black & blue top angel,
hot street sensation -.

Beut top precious one,
Paragon d' Venus-luv,
Softwalking', marvelous,
Fantastic swayin' hi-princess!
Fast action hit!

Fine faced summer beut,
Circlebigbreasted tan genius,
Hot fashion action doll!

Michael J. Phillips
Bloomington

APPROACHING A CENTURY

Tree by the river, warmed by moss,
Grown massive, wrinkled, elephantine,
Your rugged bends the long support of boys, and owls,
I see how well the sun seeks out
Your faults and furrows,
How it lights the humps and eddies of a crotch
Or notch. You are a tree of rough-ridged
Reptile finger-pathways, your skin stretched
And scarred, stiff and stubborn to the touch.
I love to round you with my hands
And sense the shape beneath,
A shape of certainty, belief;
Inside the living layer, packed with death.

Martha M. Pickrell
Elkhart

THE COACH

The coach's job is over when his team steps on the floor
He's taught them all he can and now there's nothing more

Nothing more that coach can do but watch the game from the
side
And hope his team will do things right and then he'll be sat-
isfied

Satisfied for a while, but that satisfaction won't last long
So many things to do at practice hoping nothing will go wrong

Hoping that new defense will work, hoping they'll get the of-
fense right
Hoping they'll keep working hard and get it together on game
night

When the games are over and when the season's done the
coach sits down
And thinks things over and realizes this team was number one

Maybe they didn't win a game or they weren't the best around
But it's the people they've become and the potential that's
been found

The coach only coaches players for just a few short years
And in that time the coach has seen their laughter and their
tears

The players won't play ball forever and someday they'll lose
that shooting touch
But their coach hasn't just taught them basketball, they've
learned about life and such

No, the coach's job isn't really over, even when his players
   are done for good
They might not know he really cared, but they probably should

Corri Planck
Gas City

"REUNION"

It's fun when we get together
and reminisce of days gone by
We talk about a hundred things
Of who, or which, or when, or why.

We recall things almost forgotten.
Of happy things, some are sad.
Of old friends and old neighbors
Teenage sweethearts, Mom and Dad.

Just for a while I'm transported
Back to days of yesteryears
Back to that old house in Sidney
Where I knew happiness and tears.

Then I look into a mirror
And the reflection that I see
Is not the pretty Grisso girl
Is that gray haired lady **Me??**

Now we are all grandmothers
Time has erased my youthful glow
Time has made my footsteps slower
Life grows shorter, too, I know.

So let me be just for today
A girl only in her teens.
Young and in the bloom of youth
With bright untarnished dreams.

Evelyn Pittenger
Warsaw

TRUE LOVE SHARED

A casual meeting by chance
In this fast paced world of today.
　Will our acquaintance turn from a glance
Into a friendship that will stay?

The indepth thoughts that we share
Bring us closer together with passing time.
　There are days that we think, do I dare
Trust them and expose what is on my mind.

Our hearts hold countless answers
To the never ending questions asked.
　Someday we shall master
All the fears of our past.

The future will bless our lives
With much love, hope, and trust.
　Happiness will be as vast as the skies
And our endless honesty a must.

Please let this joint effort prevail;
For a relationship like this is quite rare.
　Our feelings for one another will not fail,
Because of the true love shared.

Nita E. Pope
Peru

BATTLE ENDS

The silent wind happily
    sings through the trees.
I watched you stand before the storm,
    Your hair tossed by the breeze.

You, at the end of the cold drive way
    No more war, no more reason to be sad
A present waits for you in America-
    And she will call you "Dad."

I rush to the door in my ankle-length skirt,
    Happy and so alive and curl
My arms around your neck as if
    To ease the brutal battles you had survived.

You hold your child in front of the fireplace
    And you promise us your heart to keep.
We lay our baby in the crib for the night
    And in my arms, you cry yourself to sleep.

                Nancy S. Price
                Kokomo

I DREAM OF CHILDREN

I dream of children.
They look at me and I look back.
Each child carries a candle for it is dark.
Each child carries a different reflection in her eyes.
In their eyes, I see the sea, the sun, the sky.
I see faith, trust, and laughter.
I see peace, tenderness, and love.
They sing a soft song and they leave me.

Looking after them I hear the sound of children crying.
I see more children coming.
These have somber, tear-stained faces.
As before, each carries a candle and a reflection.
I see fear, pain, emptiness and despair.
I see rage, loneliness and lastly I see hate.
They pass on and out of sight and they go crying.

I'm crying too.
Each child I saw was me.

Barbara Pryor
Bloomington

THE FLEA CIRCUS

The flea circus is a very small but fun place to be.
I can say this because I've been there.
The things that scare them most is soapy water
    and human feet.
So if you ever come upon a flea circus, watch your
    step and don't spill any water.

Jennifer Pryor
Bloomington

APRIL STORM

The lightning dances in the skies,
And skips along while warm winds sing
In trees bent low with frightened sighs,
Against the storm that April brings.

The thunder rumbles once again,
And stills the song the cricket sings,
The petals close against the rain,
Against the storm that April brings.

The robin hovers in his nest,
And hides his head beneath his wings,
The sunbeams, equal to the test,
Wait out the storm that April brings.

The earth, washed clean, in splendor beams,
The world with sounds of new life rings,
All nature, new and reborn seems,
After the storm that April brings.

Edward Randall
Brazil

TIMES

"The times have changed", is what we hear,
"God's word is out of date".

He didn't mean that in this day we couldn't
lie and cheat and hate.

But brothers, sisters, everyone, God's word
will always stand.
And not for just a few short years,
He doesn't build on shifting sand.

A lie will always be a lie.
Won't 12 inches always make a foot?

No matter who tries to change them,
There are rules that will always stay put.

Can we change God's universal laws,
Make them fall up, instead of down?

Won't three feet always make a yard,
Can we say a square is round?

No, God's word will always stand,
Forever, and a day.

His laws still hold the stars in place,
No matter what they say!

                    Mary Redding
                    Brownsburg

SEEMINGLY LOST

Old-fashioned values,
Are seemingly lost,
Honesty fell by the way,
Pride and integrity seem to have found,
Other places to stay,
They have become passe'.

Old-fashioned values,
Where did they go?
Truth and sincerity sleep,
Honor and decency hang by a thread,
Causing us sometimes to weep.

Old-fashioned values,
Where are they now?
Do they hide within ourselves?
Just waiting to find,
An ideal time,
To grow in our hearts and minds.

Nell Reed
Hammond

"CHERRY TREE"

Ebony silhouette
on a canvas of gray,
spending eternity
poised the same way.

As seasons change
your adornment varies,
from sweet, soft petals
to bright red cherries.

How peaceful, each day must be
filled with simplistic serenity,
silently noble, in complete harmony
passing time..., a cherry tree.

                    Sheryl Elliott Reynolds
                    Carmel

RILEY REMEMBERED

I'll tell you a story of Riley
That I learned from the Palmer clan.
Uncle Ovid, a noted photographer,
Was invited to snap the man
Who was known as the "Hoosier Poet"
And also the "Children's Friend".
I don't know the length of the sitting,
But it finally came to an end.
Palmer had captured a moment
Of magic, which thousands would see:
The Poet, relaxed in his big chair,
Reading rhymes for the lads at his knee.
But after the picture was taken
The mood of enchantment was broken,
And Palmer passed on to his family
The words that the Poet had spoken.
Said Riley, the lover of childhood,
In a voice Palmer could not help hear
(No one thought that he smiled when he said it),
"Get these little brats out of here!"

Mrs. Thomas E. Rice
Lafayette

EARLY BIRD CALLS

Before break of dawn
And darkened sky;
A single bird
Begins its 'soli-cry'--
Who picks this bird
To do this task?
I ask!
Do they draw straws?
Pick a number from a hat?
What do you think of that?
Does an alarm bell ring?
To remind it to sing?
Does that first bird say--"I did it yesterday?"
Is it eeny, meeny, miny, mo?
I really want to know!
Is it, mayhap, the oldest?
Who does what it is toldest?
Or is the one chosen to greet
The bird in the "catbird" seat?
I just implore---Who picks the bird to start this chore?
Ah--perhaps it's at God's behest
To sing His praise
They sing their best!

                    Ruth Richson
                    Dupont

A PERFECT BIKE

The perfect bike comes in two shades, poppy red and azure
    blue,
for women and men.
Its Italian name, Caliente, generates appeal from the sporty-
minded or Italian descendants.
Imported from Germany by Schwinn guarantees
years of riding the open road, no matter where,
it travels.

Cushiony handlebars, black as a freshly topped driveway,
    curve
under like a contortionist from the circus.
To ones who look closely
sleek, black, rubber tires boast
a thirty-pound pressure limit for the smoothest ride
over sage roads named 139 South and 72 East.

Beyond bleached white farmhouses with giant spokes for mail-
boxes
the cornstalks stretch higher than stop signs.
Four handy brake levers allow ease in slowing
although seldom employed on this route, where chained hound
    dogs
bark hopelessly as passing cars give berth
for the cyclist to continue
on the gritty path.

Penelope A. Roa
Indianapolis

THE STORYTELLERS

The storytellers come with silver voices, songs, and ancient
    lore,
Dark and ghostly as sycamores at night reaching for the moon.
They come to schools, homes, and city festivals to
Celebrate sap rising, milk churned, and soap boiled
In black open kettles by strong-muscled country folk,
By townspeople who practice antique and auction living
Because this Indiana red barn country calls
Not only the raggedy man and the orphaned child,
But also dapper old men who slowly sip their ruby-colored
    wine,
Women who talk of books, quilts, and civic responsibilities,
Doctors, lawyers, merchants, chiefs.

The storytellers choose Riley lines and storybook characters
    and plot
A country heritage as sturdy as the seasons, teasing us with
    rhymes
And rhythms clear and clean as fresh ploughed fields.
They echo steeple chimes, tractor sounds, and courthouse
    bells
Where bold-hearted dreamers list and count the ways and
    means
Of party politics, state reforms, and global needs.
Their story-poems and lines tingle memories and comfort
Sophisticated travelers weary of the world, and we know,
In truth, in years to come, those poetry folk and vagabonds
Will visit our children's children and gladden them with
Soft easy talk, Hoosier tales, and home.

The storytellers come, and
We hear the voices of our souls.

                              Rachel Sherwood Roberts
                              Auburn

MORE THAN A DAY

'Tis a day to keep, but very much more
Than people some times on the surface see.
Keeping God's Sabbath means that we God adore
And daily pray that we may like Him be.
As a memorial of creation,
It tells whence we came and why we are here;
As a sign of sanctification,
It makes salvation through Christ very clear.
It renews our hope of eternal rest
Which the saved will enjoy in Paradise.
All who keep the Sabbath are greatly blessed
As they seek their lives with God to harmonize.
Each Sabbath kept will draw the heart nearer
To the heart of God who will become dearer.

Malinda Rodenberg
Richmond

ON SECOND THOUGHT

On the fifth day of creation
God looked down and was pleased.
He asked the angels what they thought
of course, they all agreed.
Then God paused a moment
and saw their faces all aglow.
Suddenly He wanted someone
who could tell Him no.
       SO
God went back to His world
and said "This is not the end.
I'll take another day and
make for me a friend."
Then God walked upon the earth
and picked up a lump of clay.
Into His image He shaped and molded
a man upon that day.
God gazed at His handiwork.
He really was quite pleased.
Then He breathed His spirit into man
giving him a will that's free.

Louise Rosenberry
Churubusco

THE FOXHOLE

What was he thinking in that dreadful
hour, in the mud and the heat, with his
shirt still sucking his chest like a scab?

Did he send up a prayer from the jungle,
to rise up out of the swamp like a flare?
Did he whisper his fears to the shapes

in the darkness, while small arms fire
punctured the night? Did he wonder,
at last, "Why **me?**"

Did his parents know what was happening?
What were they thinking of, during
the dinner party, while comparing vacations?

Was his dog being fed? (And what was
its name?) Was his girl going out?
Was his brother winning the big fame?

He wound himself up like a mechanical
toy spider and climbed out of his pit,
questions falling away from his mind

like a snake shedding its skin,
and the bullet buried itself in his forehead,
bouncing off the back of his skull.

He turned a perfect pirouette,
and gracefully bowed to oblivion.

Bryan Roth
Bloomington

SPRING MORN' IN INDIANA

Gentle breezes over meadows pass,
Swaying softly nimble blades of grass,
Awaken from your slumber
Forget-me-nots and feverfew
Shake off the silvery pearls of morning dew
Lift up your voice, ye robin and ye meadowlark,
Gone are the wintry days of cold and dark,
Lift up your voice, lift up your voice and sing
To greet the coming of the infant spring.

Erich William Roth
Terre Haute

FAMILY

The family is a wonderful thing to know,
they watch you play and help you grow.
They pick you up when you fall,
they're always there when you call.

If I didn't have a family to care for me,
what in the world would this life be?
The family is something we all must cherish,
for in the end we all must perish.

when we meet in the heavens above,
it will be filled with great joy and love.
So until that day comes that we must cease,
I will love you all in joy and peace.

Michael D. Royce
Indianapolis

A SATURDAY IN SEPTEMBER

The beauty of nature surrounds me,
  once the battle with dishes is won!
The leaves boast red and golden, in the lazy afternoon sun.
One bold little leaf scampers merrily, avoiding bonfires yet
  to be-
enjoying this new-found freedom from his own "family tree".
The sun has lured the crickets, too, into afternoon delight
and their chorus
                  echoes
  in my ear as it often does at night.
The resident squirrel has decided to prey upon my "little bear"
with his teasing and his mischievous ways he'll keep Gus sit-
  ting
there for hours at the base of that tree
  just waiting for the chance
                to chase him
  if he should scamper down,
  and to happily watch him dance.
Ah, but what do I see now? That wily little critter has hop-
  ped,
           limb-by-limb
         to another tree
  leaving Gus the proverbial "sitter".
Now, of old sayings, there are many and one has just come to
  me.
Would Gus simply laugh if he only knew
  he was "barking up the wrong tree"?

                  Kate Russell
                  Elkhart

DRIFTING

Sleep
Sliding slowly
And softly over
My Consciousness
Flooding my Being
With the Peace
Of the Silent Stream
Of Restfulness
Isolating my Soul
From Strife
So distant now
It seems
Like the Smooth Satin
Of the clouds' silver lining
Floating freely
To the sound
Of an Answered Prayer
Like a Whispered Secret
Settling in my Spirit
And numbing my Senses
To Life ...
A Pleasant Solitude

**Broken boldly by the Harsh Thunder
And Burning Eye of — THE TEACHER.**

Kathleen Marie Ryan
Fort Wayne

GRANDMA IN THE GIFT SHOP

Fluttering among soft folds of silk,
delicate fingers take inventory of her bodice.
Antique brooches in the showcase bring smile tugged
memories of ones she once wore
at the throat she now taps.
The glitter of jewels in the case leaps
to ignite her eyes; gaze wanders,
"What is his name?" asked shyly, as she ponders
the porcelain figure.
Lifted down from the shelf,
placed on velvet before her,
she now can stroke Oriental robed
dignity, trace long creamy beard
nudge high wrinkled forehead.
Raising parchment eyelids, she repeats politely,
"Do you know what his name is?"
"LONGEVITY" is found on the price tag.
She smiles, and greets him grandly.
Cradling him in her hand,
ignoring "C'mon!" by busy friends demanded,
she tells of moving soon to Florida:
"He should go with me, I think."
Fourteen ninety-five ransoms her new friend; longevity
leaves together, on the brink of life expanded.

                    Sara E. Sanderson
                    Indianapolis

NO PITY

I don't pity you—
   You have no sense of pride.
I will not be the one—
   To give you a free ride.
Don't wallow in self-pity—
   Hold your head up high.
Don't slither like a snake my friend—
   Spread your wings and fly!

                    Kelly Jean Sandefur
                    Indianapolis

PLAYBALL

It's a slow, grinding knuckleball.
A bayonnet twist
Vomiting mustard seared lung tissue.
One legged wine and romance, the Hun.
The psychiatrist has a breakdown.
The old man laments and is lost.
Maria remarks.
Strike one.

A fastball, inside and low.
The whine of a V2.
Ricket twisted Bataan March limbs.
Boogie woogie bullets and bombs.
Bob and Bingle keep us strong.
Rosy rivets, rubbers' scarce.
Eric and Walter are always there.
Strike two.

What a curve!
Napalm doused infants.
A police action.
Shrapnel stumps and guts by the truckload.
Convenient body counts on the nightly news.
TV death blood cartoons young children TV death blood young
    children,
66, 67, 68, 69, 70.
Strike three.

THE GAME'S NOT OVER YET!

Joseph Santo
Bloomington

NIGHTWALKING

Tonight is as Indiana
as my parents dancing
to Stardust.

Streets are midwestern
and humid.

I walk.
Memories pool
in alleyways.

I have been a
smalltown girl
for 34 years.

East coast friends
say Hoosier blood is
too thick.

I say,
listen,
as the whistle rush
of an Indiana train
walks me
back home again.

Barbara J. Schwegman
Bloomington

PROMISE

Wondrously wrought, intricately fashioned,
A gleaming, golden door
Stands between all the beautiful things
My longing heart yearns for
And me.

there are a few small openings
Arranged in its design--
The tiny glimpses of beauty are held
Close to this heart of mine.

A canvas touched by paint and brush
Held in a Master's hand
Reveals a sunset on wave-washed beach
Of burnished, golden sand
To me.

Myriads of bows drawn lovingly
A cross unnumbered strings--
To this with pure and unmixed joy
My hungry, needy soul clings.

The door still stands unmoveable,
And yet it lets me hear
Angelic voices singing heavenly music
From some far-distant sphere
For me.

                    Eileen Sexton
                    Knox

LITTLE GIRL

A little girl is just the thrill to set my heart awhirl.
She loves to hug me and to bug me quite frequently, alter-
nately as she will, and to show her how much I care I must
do secretly cuz it is almost a downright outrage to love a
child so much, but I can't help it. I just can't stop it,
she melts my heart with a touch.

                              Terri Sharp
                              Marion

OUR WONDERFUL YEARS

True love comes but once in life
A pure sweet girl becomes your wife
Your home and children, complete the plan
So clasp it tightly while you can.

For all too soon the years pass by
The children gone, just you and I
Then come the winters of our years
Forgetting life's unhappy tears
We devote ourselves to one another
Just you grandfather and I, grandmother.

G. Marie Siler
Marion

MEMORIES

Once, with boldness born of youth
I dared to dream the world was mine,
Each dawn a stepping stone of hope
To treasure 'till the end of time;
Horizons beckoned, rainbow-hued,
And lured me on - love waited there
To gift my heart with happiness,
A lifelong legacy to share.
Fate showered us with golden moments
Unaware, my love and I,
That sadness sometimes clouds the way
And youth looks back to wonder why.
From echoes of remembrance
Grief is tempered day by day
With little seeds of kindness sown
That flower where I make my way;
For love once nurtured never dies,
In memory it multiplies.

Elizabeth M. Singleton
Decatur

GOING HOME ON MOTHER'S DAY

Just as we honor our modern heros,
Honor to mother we all must pay,
No one ever deserved it any more,
SO GO ON HOME, IT'S MOTHER'S DAY.

She was a good Christian mother,
A treasure no money could buy,
She was kinder & wiser than most,
A little timid and a little shy.

Mother really loved her children,
She would always call to say,
Now kids you know I love you,
SO GO HOME, IT'S MOTHER'S DAY

How precious are all my memories,
Of our family so happy and gay,
All dressed up in our Sunday best,
And going home on Mother's Day.

Mother's life will soon be over,
One day she'll hear her Savior say,
My dear child you know I love you,
SO COME ON HOME, IT'S MOTHER'S DAY.

Gladys Smallwood
Richmond

ECONOMY MEASURE

Father bought two piglets to save money.
Footballs with stubby legs, flat snouts, curled tails,
They were to eat scraps, grow large, provide meat.
We named them Sara and Sally.

When I forgot to feed them,
They came rooting and snorting to the back door.
We greeted them as family friends,
And fed them from our hands.

When father had them slaughtered,
The house was quiet, cold, lonely.
If you want to enjoy the pork,
Don't name the pigs.

                    Henry V. Smith
                    Bloomington

FREE

I looked up the word for "retire" to see
If the Dictionary said what it means to me
"To retire from duty", it says right there,
That I did without a care.
For workday problems---Leave me be,
My definition: I just call it "FREE"!
Free to go any day of the week,
A short trip, a long one, or just to seek;
A visit with friends, a trip to the Zoo,
Time with the grandchildren, or something new.
No more rush; get up when you please; stay up late,
No early work date; No pressure from bosses,
Who must make their way; Just finish now, or put off
    for some other day.

I love it, I love it, so glad to be free
Maybe ten minutes I missed it, the stress and the strain,
Now it's my own, no more man-made pain.
I highly suggest the life that I lead;
For those soon to join this band of many,
Hear me, take heed, there's joy aplenty.
I'm free to be, just do for me,
or at my will, for others, I'LL JUST BE FREE!

                Virginia S. Smith
                Merrillville

KUMA

she met the swaying and the black rolling
of the Danube under that moonless sky in '46.
the wetness of that river so cold
threatened to fill her lungs
with icy blue nails
but water, no, time could no longer taunt
her want of the newness
on the other side, and the alone.
the river knows nothing but that.
and along with its piercing cold
touches her deep and promises
to chill despair of the dead now behind.
her parents not crying but hoping
and pushing her along.
no longer a feeble struggle
her pupils explode in the night
and she swims faster along and away
from the barren shore
closing and closer to that other side
where what the river knows
waits like a warm fire
to pick her up and take her home.

                    Lillian Sorak
                    Bloomington

THOUGHTS ON WHEN THE LIGHTS WENT OUT

I fear
far meaner wolves
than those
that eye me hungrily
behind thin walls --
beyond the range
of my capacity.

I fear
far meaner wolves...

I fear
the fatted dogs --
the ones
that sneak about my feet
with barleyed breath
and lick away
my thumbs when I'm asleep.

Emily Spindler
Russiaville

THE HARVEST MOON

The Harvest Moon is shining
O'er all the World to-night
Come, let us gather Harvest
In the full Moonlight.

We will gather pumpkins
And shock the yellow corn.
Come, let us be merry
While the Harvest Moon is on.

Come, let us have a quilting party
Also a spelling bee.
Test your strength at log rolling
How merry we will be.

We shall have some cider
And pumpkin pie too.
Come, let us be merry
Now is the Harvest Moon.

Come, let's play in the Moonlight
Down through the Harvest field.
Dancing and merrily singing
Before the cold we feel.

And while the Moon is shining
O'er all the World to-night.
Come, let us be happy and gay
In the Harvest full Moonlight.

Charles Cecil Staggs
Terre Haute

FAITH

God's ballet on our kitchen floor,
Through a windowpane from leaves, sunshine and wind,
Dancing in an unknown pattern,
Never to be seen again.
No man can duplicate what God has done this
short time--with leaves, wind and sunshine,
And if it is as beautiful tomorrow as it is today,
Perhaps God will do it again, who on earth can say.
So I'll just sit and wait here in this place,
And there before my eyes,
Is God's ballet again.

James R. Stevenson
Franklin

UNTIL THE END OF TIME

I cannot let the tears fall,
But, my heart is aching so.
I see your face.
Your smile.
Your eyes.
But, I can't let you know.

I can still feel your touch.
Your lips gently pressing mine.
And I will love you,
My own true love,
Until the end of time.

I no longer will see you,
Or hear your voice.
Or see your beautiful eyes shine.
But, I will love you,
My own true love,
Until the end of time.

My dreams are gone.
They left with you.
My days and nights drag by.
But, I will love you,
My own true love,
Until the end of time.

Nancy Stewart-Tornai
Whiting

THE LOVE OF RILEY

Back in 1928 in my home town
In the Rockies high in the sky,
James Whitcomb Riley was loved
The same as any other guy.

His poems were read and recited
For occasions of every kind.
We 7th graders performed and mimicked
All the Riley poems that we could find.

"This is the way you look," Ruth said,
As she drew her face all out of shape,
Her fingers tucked up her nose,
Her eyes blaring and her mouth agape.

And how we laughed and laughed
About the pesky little fly
Who flitted form the backhouse
To Grandma's cherry pie.

Yes, we loved his books of poetry,
And admired his humor so keen;
But, little did I know then
I would be moving to his scene,

From the Colorado mountains
Under the Pike's Peak Dome,
To rear my wonderful family
In Huntington, my Indiana Home.

G. L. Stouffs
Huntington

PICTURE POEMS

Poems written by Riley I've been reading tonight
As I ponder his thoughts trying to gain some insight
What kind of a man was he?
This man, Mr. James Whitcomb Riley
A poet by trade;
But, with his words, a picture was made
Inside my mind into the past I could be,
For awhile, but now it's back to the future for me
For life in Indiana's much more hectic today
But, because of his poems I can truly say
I felt the warmth and the charm of Hoosiers from yesteryear
As his poems created pictures that brought both a smile and
    a tear
I finally decided an artist he must be
For this man with his words painted pictures for me!

                    Narda Rae Strong
                    Churubusco

CALYPSO

Within the bleak young man awaits-
    Without, the festival rages.
The throbbing tunes blare through the walls
    Its crashing din on all who fall
    And cringe in metal cages.

    Its rhythm is contagious.

Why was this man selected over
    the others of his kind-
Was he abnormally perverse
    and graphic in his mind?
Cast the first stone if you wish
    And there you thus will find

    Your own sins well-defined.

So dance on, dance on, you renegades
    in mad calypso beat
And cheer the death of criminals
    While you hope God delete
Your transgressions from His memory
    And make your souls complete.

    (For that is quite a feat!)

                Lynda Sweetman
                Jeffersonville

ALLELU'

A tumble of thunder
    And a sparkle of rain
Nudged our tired, brown grass--
    Allelu'--green again!

Lawrence L. Vaughn Thompson
Crawfordsville

WINTER WOOD

Something dies in a crowded wood
Barren limbs, silhouette on white
The cycle of life becomes a god.

The wind and chill scourges as it would
Becomes the enemy for a life to fight
Something dies in a crowded wood.

An evergreen bough affords a hood
For a vagrant beast to stay a night
The cycle of life becomes a god.

Snow stained crimson with the blood
Salvation's sacrifice to the might
Something dies in a crowded wood.

Who determines as someone should
Whose life is precious and worth the fight
The cycle of life becomes a god.

Apathetic to man, that's nature's mood
But in man to man lies hope for right
Something dies in a crowded wood
The cycle of life becomes a god.

                    Mitzi Thomas
                    Upland

WRITER'S CRAMP

Writer's Cramp is frustration itself
As the writer's mind and his pen remain on the shelf.
His soul aches for the thoughts of the wise.
But, only in time can he write the line
To explain the feelings he hides.

Please don't be mistaken
Of the toll it has taken
On his dreams, his schemes and his years.
And his hopes he holds high, but his dreams will die
Unless he has conquered his fears.

Yes, his pen has been lazy --
He's convinced he's gone crazy
By letting his pen lie still.
But, awake now in the night, he's beginning to write,
And he knows that he always will.

And yes to be sure --
There's prob'ly no cure
For the thoughts that explode in his mind.
And he hopes that some day his words drift your way,
And you'll bury them to treasure in time.

                    Joel Thorne
                    Marion

FOR JAMES WHITCOMB RILEY

in summer
you are cousin
to silver cricket call
in fields
beneath the dreaming moon

in autumn
you are will-o'-the-wisp
poplar leaf
dropping down
the gold-winged wind

in winter
your feelings
are quick and live
as sparrow song
in the blue-green spruce

in spring
your heart
is a handful of flowers
in the gaze
of wondering children

Charles B. Tinkham
Hammond

BUTTERFLY

Ben found a tiger swallowtail.
Bright yellow wings, edged in carbon black,
black stripes through the yellow,
trailing back from the front edges,
like a tiger's stripes, someone must have thought.
Along the black margins
are small yellow spots and crescents.
Black veins cross and join the black stripes
on the front wings.
Underneath the rear wings are daubs of orange
and iridescent blue.
Ben said it was dead,
and set it on a stool by the front door.
When I sat down I saw it move
so slightly.
Not dead yet, Ben.
What's wrong with it?
I don't know.
Such a beautiful thing,
lying there, wings spread, perfect but
barely moving.
Sometimes you can see
the small, delicate details of a thing
only when it's dead,
or barely moving.

Thomas R. Tokarski
Bloomington

CITY OF DREAMS

City of love, city of lights,
City of maybes, city of mights,
A place apart, a place above,
A place to find an endless love.

City of hatred, city of blight,
Devoid of feeling, devoid of light,
A place beyond your wildest fears,
A place of pain and endless tears.

And so it is in the city of dreams,
A place of laughter, a place of screams,
A place for wonder, a place for pity,
And so it is in this wondrous city.

Jerry Lee Tomblin
North Judson

FLOWING SANDS

Gather ye rosebuds while ye may,
Old time is still a-flying,
and this same flower that smiles to-day,
To-morrow may be dying.

To-day is ours; why do we fear?
To-day is ours; we have it here:
Let's banish business, banish sorrow:
Because to God belongs to-morrow.

Time is too slow for those who wait,
too swift for those who fear,
too long for those who grieve,
too short for those who rejoice,
but for those who love ...
Time is eternity.

The sands of time shall flow upon the barren land,
the sands of time shall flow, be it for woman or man,
at first it seems to hesitate as if not knowing which way to
   flow,
as life progresses its downward path it's found its way to go,

it picks up speed with family gone or friends so far between,
when trying to stop the onward rush of lonely years it's seen,
to open the door to companionship and love with fellow man,
the only thing that stops the clock and slows the flowing sand.

                    Charlie Towles
                    Connersville

HOMAGE TO JIM

Friend, just mention old Jim Riley,
Then the long-gone days of yore
Return again, and one grown old
is back on childhood's shore.

There the face of first-grade teacher,
There that first-grade sweetheart, too
How clear the faces of old friends
And schoolmates, in review!

There, knee-deep in joyous June-time
And stone-bruised on toe and heel,
That swimmin'-hole we haunt again;
That carefree spirit feel.

Oh, those days of sacred splendor,
How the meadow's diamond-dew
Would sparkle in the dawn's first light,
And wink at me and you!

When October came a flashin',
In her red and golden smock,
A tossin' tangy Injun-haze
'Round every fodder-shock!

Ah, that Greenfield-rhymer Riley,
That old Hoosier-Poet near
To childhood and to hearth and home,
Could set it down so clear.

That, to those of us who learned him
And his dialect and rhyme,
To heart and soul, the joy he brings
Shall be for all life's time.

Yes, just mention old Jim Riley
And the scenes of yesteryear
Come rushing back, to one now old,
And childhood's--very near!

Norman V. Ulery (deceased)
Bloomington

THE RESCUE

Once again I nauseate myself.
The words come out jet-propelled
like vomit. I have no control,
but I continue to talk, hoping
that the words will line up like
good soldiers and take orders.
Either they do not recognize my au-
thority or do not understand me.
I bob for brains like a soon-to-be-
beached whale afloat on a scummy
sea, but I do not give up--cannot.
A woman with wit butts in. I am
her grateful slave, and while search-
ing for a way to express my regard,
I try to swallow my beasty tongue,
my now dumbstruck heart clumsy
with love, inarticulate with ardor.

David Vancil
Terre Haute

GENESIS

Your door stood ajar,
morning fog
trying a thumb
upon the cold latch.
My mind blown open
by fresh winds
heard Gypsy chords
riding on the dawn.
Curiously I came
past the sill
thru golden motes
or umber shadows.
This quiet haven
boldly held
in mellow wood
and pewter glow
hints of more to come,
one small smile
cupping a flame
will forever burn.

Ivan Wampler
Dublin

DAFFODIL DREAMS

When Mama was little
she picked daffodils to ship on the Gary train.

Gary.

Her Daddy told her rich people in Gary would
buy daffodils from street vendors
because they had no flower fields of their own.

Her dreams then were water-colored,
pastel yellow and pure white, precious bright isles in a sea
of green.

Dreams watered with the sticky essence
of newly-plucked stems,
early morning dew.

And waking in the morning to pick daffodils,
she'd feel good to ship her dreams to
people who might not have any of their own.

The other day, I stopped on the street
and paid for bunches of daffodils.

Their sweet dew trickled through my fingers,
lifted my hopes to pasted yellow and pure white.

An armload of dreams from Mama.

                    Tara J. Williams
                    Brazil

A MOTHER'S DAY MESSAGE

...One can't even begin to imagine just
how painful life would "Be",
If there wasn't ever that special person
called "Mother" for you, nor me.
A mother is comforting in helping one
to overcome the many trials of this world.
...Even from the beginning of time, when
God created Adam, he knew that Adam
would be lonely, so he created Eve.
God extended his mercy throughout
history...
...so for every child that is conceived,
there is a mother-to-be.
My message for all mankind to read
for that "special" person, known as
mother, whether she's with you or not.
Honor her by wearing your "red or
white".
A Mother is a Gift of Love, from
God!!!

Rita J. Wise
Indianapolis

MY FATHER

when this was our kind of
grey day
you were king of pancakes
we knew your love
butter melting through us
under your sun

on this kind of day
with wet leaves stuck to me
the windows dark with syrup
I look in

how goes the griddle?
the smoke still smells like breakfast
things are a little different
but my stomach never lies

I recognize the house
can you see me through the yellowed light?
the molasses mask has holes, Dad
but
there's something young out here

W. T. Yanikoski
Walkerton

"SPRING BREEZE"

Blow, zephyr, blow
And toss the cotton clouds
Along the deep blue sky-way
And test the sinew of the trees
Struggling for balance in your breath
And push the jacketed boy along
Who loses his cap and chases it
Laughing down the street.

Philip H. Young
Speedway

SUMMER'S END

An autumn leaf is floating
    through the air
On a cool
    gentle
        afternoon breeze
The only sound there is
Is the song of the wind
    as it flows
        briskly
Through the branches of the trees

As I sit here
    leaning against a tree
I think of my most cherished past
    the times I'll never see again
And I have to laugh
    about the times I've had
And I sigh
    as it comes to summer's end

                    Jenni Zapf
                    Greenfield